James Porter

Observations on the Religion, Law, Government, and Manners, of the Turks

James Porter

Observations on the Religion, Law, Government, and Manners, of the Turks

ISBN/EAN: 9783337310707

Printed in Europe, USA, Canada, Australia, Japan

Cover: Foto ©Suzi / pixelio.de

More available books at **www.hansebooks.com**

OBSERVATIONS

ON THE RELIGION,

LAW, GOVERNMENT,

AND MANNERS,

OF THE TURKS.

VOL. I.

——fas fit mihi vifa referre. OVID. Ep. xvi.

LONDON,

Printed for J. NOURSE, Bookfeller to His MAJESTY.

MDCCLXVIII.

CONTENTS.

CHAP.

———————

ERRATA.

Notes, Page 54. *Inftead of* in the Turkifh courts by Hanifa,—*read*, in the Turkifh courts, written by Hafne.

Line 5. p. 62. *Inftead of* he therefore very artfully framed it after the prototypes of truth,—*read*, he therefore very artfully took for its prototype, truth itfelf—the Mofaic and Chriftian revelations.

Line 2. p. 64. *Inftead of* the vifiting of the Moth, *read*, the vifiting of the morn.

Page 101. Note to be added—The *Boftangi Pafha* always fteers the Sultan's boat ; he is the chief of the *Boftangees*, or gardeners, who, on occafion, form a confiderable military corps. The *Seliftar Aga* is the Sultan's fword-bearer, and conftantly attends him.

Page 113. in the laft line, *for* Mehemet Ragib *read*, Ragib Mehemet Pafha.

OBSERVATIONS, &c.

CHAP. I.

The Difficulty of obtaining information in Turky.—Character of the Turks.

WRITERS who never ſtirred out of their own * country, and travellers who have run † over immenſe regions with haſty and tranſitory pace, have given us long ac-

* Thevenot, librarian to the French king, was never out of Europe. Gemelli Carreri, a Neapolitan gentleman, who, for many years, never quitted his chamber, during a long indiſpoſition, amuſed himſelf with writing a voyage round the world ; giving characters of men, and deſcriptions of countries, as if he had actually viſited them.

† Tournefort, Paul Lucas, Pocock, &c.

B   counts

counts of various countries and people; evidently collected from the idle report and abfurd tradition of the ignorant vulgar, from whom only they can have received thofe relations, which we fee heaped together with fo undifcerning a credulity.

The Turks have abundantly fhared this treatment: without taking notice therefore of what even the moft correct writers may have faid, I fhall throw out, fo far as reached my own knowledge, fome fhort obfervations and general ftrictures on the religion, law, government, and manners of that people. If what I advance has no other merit, it will at leaft have that of being ftrictly true.

It is extremely difficult to come at information in Turky; enquiries give
dif-

difguft. The Mahomedan law is fo ftrict and pofitive, that it confines, and binds the underftanding of its fectaries within the narrow limits of what the *Koran* teaches; and renders them inconverfible with the reft of mankind; efpecially on the fubject of religion, or of their own cuftoms. Strangers who do not, and cannot perfectly underftand the language, muft converfe by interpreters; but thefe dare not enter into enquires they think will give the leaft offence: on thefe fubjects therefore, they never do, nor will interpret; if put to it, evafion is their refuge, and both the queftion they make, and anfwer they return you, will be merely their own.

It may then be afked, how are we to be informed in Turky? I muft anfwer, very imperfectly. A long and

conti-

continued practice in that country, many connections and dependencies amongst different ranks of people, may, by mere chance, lead us to some truth; but certain it is, that we have hitherto very imperfect accounts of their religion or of their manners.

To trace correctly the mere outline of any national character, is, I am sensible, a difficult task; of the Turks it is peculiarly so: I shall nevertheless make the attempt.

The Turks are in general a sagacious, thinking people; in the pursuit of their own interest, or fortune, their attention is fixt on one object, and they persevere with great steadiness until they attain their purpose. They are in common life seemingly obliging and humane, not without appearances

of

of gratitude : perhaps all or either of thefe, when extended towards Chriftians, are practifed with a view of fome advantage. Intereft is their fupreme good; where that becomes an object of competition, all attachment of friendfhip, all ties of confanguinity are diffolved; they become defperate, no barrier can ftop their purfuit, or abate their rancour towards their competitors. In their demeanor they are rather hypochondriac, grave, fedate, and paffive; but when agitated by paffion, furious, raging, ungovernable; big with diffimulation; jealous, fufpicious †, and vindictive beyond

---

* The Zonanas, famous Jews, refiding at Conftantinople, are purveyors to the whole body of Janiffaries throughout the empire; receive all their monies, fupply them with all neceffaries, advance cafh to their (a) *Agas*, to all their officers, and even to the common men.

(a) Generals—or commandants.

con-

conception; perpetuating revenge from generation to generation. In matters

The father of the prefent Zonana had the fame employment; he lived to a very advanced age, in high reputation, and had acquired great weight and influence with that turbulent, formidable corps. Tiriacki Mehemet Pafcha, who, in 1746, had the feals conferred on him as Vizir, raifed himfelf from a low beginning: two and twenty years before he attained his dignity, he was an ordinary *Katib*, or fcribe, to that militia; at which time, on fome difpute of intereft with Zonana, he declared, with violent affeveration, that if he ever had it in his power, Zonana's fhould be the firft head he would ftrike off: in effect, he had been but a few days Vizir, before he executed his purpofe; time could not mitigate his revenge; he took the old man's head off even at the rifk of his own fecurity; for fo great was the affection the Janiffaries bore Zonana, it was thought this act of violence might caufe a rebellion.

Turks have been known to come from the frontiers of Perfia, into Afia minor, and Thrace, to revenge the death of a grandfather, uncle, or coufin, many years after the offence has been committed; it is ufual for the parent to remind his child, the uncle his ne-

of

of religion, tenacious, fupercilious, and morofe.

phew, of any injury their family or relations have fuffered, and excite them continually to revenge. I wifh it were not true, that in many of the Greek iflands, among thofe who call themfelves Chriftians, the fame practice was not prevalent.

The chriftian *Drugomen*, or interpreters, are uncommonly generous to the meaneft, the moft indigent Turk, treating them with deference and politenefs: when the reafon is afked, they tell you, they have feen fo many, from the very loweft, rife to the higheft ftations, that it is neceffary to guard againft their revenge; in truth they fear them; education and obfervation lead them to it.

B 4 CHAP.

C H A P. II.

Of the Mahomedan religion—and the pilgrimage to Mecca.

AMONG the many fingular and whimfical conceits of a * modern writer, we meet with pertinent remarks and fhrewd obfervations, not always indeed merely his own; he tells us, " that " to judge properly of a religion, we " muft not take it from the books of " thofe who profefs it; we muft fee " how it is practifed in a country " where it is eftablifhed, to know what " it is; we fhall there find it a very " different thing : each has its tradi- " tions, peculiar interpretations, cuf- " toms, prejudices; thefe make the " very effence of their faith, and thefe

* J. J. Rouffeau, Em. liv. iv.

" muft

" muſt be combined with what their
" books profeſs, before we can be able
" to judge of it."

To aſcertain, therefore, the true
ſpirit of Mahomedaniſm, we muſt appeal to an impartial obſervation, of the
real influence it has on the practice of
its followers.

The Mahomedan belief at firſt ſight
appears extremely ſimple : what they
firſt require from a proſelyte to their
religion, is ſolely the repetition of a
ſhort creed : *Allah il Allah, Muhamed
reſoul Allah* ; that is, " There is but
" one God, and Mahomet is his pro-
" phet." He is then confirmed by
ablution and a ſhort prayer, and thus
received into the number of true believers. Circumciſion generally follows,

Hence

HENCE fome have pretended, and many might be led to think, that it is a religion by no means clafhing violently with reafon; the great bafis on which it is founded, being the unity of the Deity.

BUT this plaufible initiation is only a firft ftep, from whence the convert muft plunge into the belief of all the abfurdities of the *Koran*, every article of which he muft receive as revelation from God, written in heaven, and fent down by the Almighty in mercy to his chofen people; he muft firmly believe that repeating this revelation fo many times a year, obferving rigoroufly the faft of *Ramazan*, performing ablutions on different parts of the body,

---

* A *Reis Effendi*, or fecretary of ftate, reputed of great ability and learning, fent for a chriftian *Drugoman*, or interpreter, on very ur-

care-

carefully extending them to certain exact spaces and critical proportions;
going the pilgrimage to Mecca; drinking a potion of water, in which their
prophets old robe✝ has been dipt; repeating some, or the whole, of the
ninety-nine names of the different at-
tributes of the Deity, on a string of
ninety-nine beads; are all devotional
duties, so essentially necessary to a true
believer, that without them the purest
heart and the sincerest faith are insuf-
ficient to recommend him to divine fa-

gent busness; he attended, and found the secretary deeply engaged in dispute with his
son-in-law on the important question, to what
exact height their hands or arms, feet or legs,
should be washed, to render themselves truly acceptable to God?

✝ The Grand Signor is guardian of this
robe, he himself distributes the water annually after the *Beiram*, in small phials to all his
courtiers, and they to their followers and
friends.

your;

vour; thefe practices he likewife holds to be the efficacious and the indifpenfible means, by which to atone for all his crimes and immoralities.

Such abfurdities might be looked on, as inventions contrived by Mahomet, merely to amufe and catch his ignorant and fimple followers. They would indeed be of little confequence to the moral order of the world, if the conclufions drawn from them by the Turks, were not, in the higheft degree, injurious to the reft of mankind: for, hence they deduce, that all who are not of their belief, and embrace not the doctrines of their prophet, are ⁕ objects of Divine vengeance and abhorrence; confequently, of their deteftation, on whom they are to exercife violence, fraud, and rapine.

⁕ Koran, Sale's Edit. chap. iii. p. 50. chap. v. p. 83.

The

THE force and efficacy of this principle operates fo effectually, that Mahomedans are ever ready to demonftrate their zeal by fpurning on the
perfons, ravifhing the property, and
even deftroying the very exiftence of
thofe who profefs a different religion.
Afk them ; let them be candid and
fpeak plain, they will frankly confefs,
that fuch is their duty, fo they are
commanded, and that they are con-
vinced it is moft meritorious in the
fight of God and his prophet.

THEIR fuperior thirft for gold is the
potent prefervative of thofe Chriftians
and Jews who live amongft them.
Thefe are an inexhauftible treafure to
government; a fource conftantly flowing to fupply the wants of multitudes,
even of the powerful and the ambitious : hence therefore, religious tyranny

and

and the inveterate prejudice of enthuſiaſm, are in ſome ſort ſubdued and vanquiſhed.

THE firſt effort of Mahomedan education is to root deep in the minds of their children, a high contempt of all other religions; from babes they are carefully taught to diſtinguiſh them by the opprobrious name of *Giaur*, or Infidel.

THE habit becomes ſo forcible by the time they are men, that they can uſe no other term; they follow them with it in every ſtreet, and will often affect puſhing againſt them with the utmoſt contempt.

MEN of dignity, or thoſe of a rank above the populace, behave with ſeeming courteſy and complaiſance, though often

often with a fort of ftern fuperiority;
but you are fcarce difmiffed, however
civilly, before they will honour you
with the high title of *Dumus*, or hog,
the animal they hold the moft odious,
deteftable, and impure of the whole
creation.

TAKE the moft miferable Turk dependant on a Chriftian, one who lives
by him, would ftarve without him;
let the Chriftian require of him the
falute of peace, the *Salem Alek*, or,
" Peace be with you," he would fooner
die than give it; he would think himfelf abominated by God, and that his
prophet would look down on him with
indignation as an infidel and apoftate;
it is referved folely for Muffulmen,
true believers. The utmoft they dare
fay, and many of them think it faying
too much, is *Chair olla*, " Good be
with you."

THEY

THEY are enjoined by their religion
to extend it by making converts ; and
to prefs all thofe of any other, at leaft
three times to embrace it. Some affect a forcible and unbecoming zeal ;
others more moderate, content themfelves with a mere formal requifition ;
but either of them will change their
tone, according as they conceive the
perfon they addrefs may be ufeful to
them or not.

THEY cannot reject the moft abject
or * wicked mortal, who offers to become a true believer, though they
know his crimes, and that he is wholly
ignorant of what their belief confifts in.

† The real worth of *pafhawlycks*, or
governments, are in proportion to the

* A profeft and notorious murderer, ignorant of their language.
† Between Conftantinople and Angoura, in
number

number of the Chriſtian inhabitants, becauſe the paſhaws may with them indulge all their luſt of power, their zeal and avarice ; tyrannize, harraſs, oppreſs, and ſuck their very vitals ; from them they fear no complaints.

Aſia Minor, above three or four hundred villages have been, in a ſpace of years, abandoned by their Chriſtian inhabitants. About Aleppo, and other parts of Syria, greater numbers, much later, have been deſerted. Theſe miſerable Chriſtians do not quit the empire, but emigrate into cities, or wherever elſe they imagine themſelves leſs expoſed to oppreſſion and diſtreſs.

It is but a few years ago, that all the Greek inhabitants of the Morea joined in an *Arz mabzar*, or general repreſentation, againſt their paſhaw ; the oppreſſion and extortions were enormous : the paſhaw brought the Turkiſh inhabitants for evidences in his favour ; and though he had ruined a multitude of Greeks, their complaints were not the immediate cauſe of his removal.

Hence it is, that the moſt opulent Greeks ſecure their property, and often their perſons, at Venice : numbers of them are always reſident there.

C　　　　　　　But

But they cherish and spare those of their own religion: and they, when any Christian representations of a Pashaw's misconduct reach the Porte, are sure evidence in his favour.

But such evidence, though it serves the turn, is believed by nobody; facts are evident and incontestible: reside at Constantinople, observe the continual fear Christians and Jews live in; the means they use to obtain protection from the Turks in power; the enormous villanies they seem under the necessity of perpetrating on each other, as the price of that favour; the wrongs, violences, and insults they are daily labouring under, and obliged passively to bear; you will thence form a true idea of Mohamedanism, and a just estimate of the influence it has on the manners of its votaries.

THERE

THERE is no command in the *Koran* more energetic, nor held in greater respect by Muffulmen, than the pilgrimage to Mecca. A *hadgi*, or pilgrim is always reckoned regenerate; he who has not been there, laments, he deplores his own fituation in life, which has not permitted him to perform this duty; and is anxious for the ftate of his foul. This pilgrimage is, indeed, the main bafis of Mahomedanifm; for whoever performs it methodically, and omits not any part, is confident he recommends himfelf effectually to the favour of God, that he is abfolved from all fin, and rendered permanently acceptable to him.

SINCE, therefore, an exact account of all a Turk performs at Mecca, muft give us as true an idea of the Mahomedan religion, as if we beheld their

practice;

practice; this pilgrimage being their main route to falvation; I fhall exhibit a fhort hiftory of it, extracted from the journal of a true Muffulman, who feems to have noted down every part as foon as he had performed it.

' After the month of their faft, or
' the *Ramazan*, the caravan of Damaf-
' cus, compofed of the pilgrims from
' Europe and Afia Minor, the Arabi-
' an, and the principal one from Cai-
' ro, fet out for Mecca. They all have
' their ftated time of departure, and
' their regular ftages. That from Cairo
' begins the journey thirty days after
' Ramazan; and the conductors fo re-
' gulate each day's march, that they
' arrive in forty days; that is, juft be-
' fore the *Corban*, or great *Beiram* of
' facrifice.

' Five

'Five or six days before that festi-
'val, the three caravans, confisting of
'about 200,000 men, and 300,000
'beasts of burthen, unite and encamp
'at some miles from Mecca.

'The pilgrims form themselves into
'small detachments, and enter the
'town to perform the ceremonies pre-
'paratory to that great one of sacri-
'fice. They are led through a street
'of continual ascent, until they arrive
'at a gate on an eminence, called the
'Gate of Health; from thence they
'see the great mosche, which enclofes
'the house of Abraham; they salute
'it with the profoundest devotion,
'repeating twice, *Salem Alek Irufoul*
'*Alla*; that is, " Peace be with the
"Ambaffador of God." 'Thence,
'at some distance, they mount up five
'steps, to a large platform faced with

C 3   'stone,

' ftone, where they offer up their pray-
' ers. Then they defcend on the other
' fide of it, and advance towards two
' fimilar arches, at fome diftance from
' each other, which they pafs thro' with
' great filence and devotion. This cere-
' mony muft be performed feven times.

' FROM hence they proceed to the
' great mofche which enclofes the houfe
' of Abraham ; enter the mofche, and
' walk feven times round the little
' building contained within it ; fay-
' ing, " This is the houfe of God,
" and of his fervant Abraham ;" then
' kiffing with great reverence * a black

* This ftone, our Muffulman tells us, fell from
heaven, accompanied with a voice, faying,
" Wherever this ftone falls, there you muft
" build the houfe of God, and from that houfe
" he will hear the prayers of finners." That
on its defcent it was as white as fnow, and is
become black from the touch of fuch a number
of finful lips ; for the pilgrims are obliged to
' ftone,

' stone, said to be descended white
' from heaven, they go to the famous
' well called † *Zun-Zun*, and plunge
' into it with all their cloaths, continu-
' ally repeating *Toba Alla, Toba Alla,*
" Forgiveness God, Forgiveness God."

' THEY then drink a draught of that
' fetid turbid water, and depart.

' THE duty of bathing and drinking
' they are obliged to pass through once;
' but those who will gain paradise be-
' fore the others, must perform it once
' a day, during the stay of the caravan.

' AT fifteen miles from the town of
' Mecca, there is a hill, or small
' mountain, called *Ghiabal Arafata,* or,

kiss it, otherwise they cannot be cleared of their
sins.

† This well the angel shewed Agar when
she was distressed in the desert, and found no
water for her son Ishmael; it is called by the
Arabs, *Zem-Zem.*

C 4   " The

" The Mount of Forgivenefs;" it is
' about two miles in circumference,
' a moft delicious fpot; on it Adam
' and Eve met, after the Lord, for
' their tranfgreffion, had feparated them
' forty years ; here they cohabited,
' and lived in excefs of happinefs,
' having built a houfe on this mount,
' called *Beith Adam*, i. e. Adam's
' Houfe. The night before, or the eve
' of the day of facrifice, the three ca-
' ravans, each ranged in a triangular
' form, circumviron this mountain;
' during this whole night the people
' rejoice, clamour, and riot, fire cannon,
' mufkets, piftols, and fire-works, with
' the continued noife of drums and
' trumpets. On the day, a profound
' filence fucceeds, they flay their fheep,
' offer up their facrifice on the moun-
' tain, with all the demonftrations of
' the moft profound devotion.

' On

' On a fudden a fcheik, or fantone,
' rufhes from amidft them, mounted
' on his camel, he afcends five fteps,
' rendered practicable for that purpofe,
' and in a fet fermon preaches to the
' people.'

" Return praife and thanks for the
" infinite and immenfe benefits given
" by God to Mahometans, through
" the mediation of his moft beloved
" friend and prophet Mahomet; for
" that he has delivered them from the
" flavery and bondage of fin and ido-
" latry in which they were plunged;
" has given them the houfe of Abra-
" ham, from whence they can be
" heard, and their petitions granted.
" Alfo the Mountain of Forgivenefs,
" by means of which they can im-
" plore him, and obtain pardon and
" remiffion of all their fins.

" For

" For that the bleſſed, pious, and
" merciful God, giver of all good
" gifts, commanded his ſecretary Abra-
" ham to build himſelf a houſe at
" Mecca, whence his deſcendants
" might pray to him, the Almighty,
" and their deſires be fulfilled.

" On this command, all the moun-
" tains in the world ran, as it were,
" each ambitious to aſſiſt the ſecretary
" of the Lord, and to furniſh a ſtone
" towards erecting the holy houſe;
" all except this poor little mountain,
" which, through mere indigence,
" could not contribute a ſtone, it con-
" tinued therefore thirty years griev-
" ouſly afflicted; at length, the eter-
" nal God obſerved its anguiſh, and
" moved with pity at its long ſuffer-
" ing, broke forth, ſaying, I can for-
" bear no longer, my child, your bit-

" ter

" ter lamentations have reached my
" ears, and I now declare, that all
" thofe who henceforth come to vifit
" the houfe of my friend Abraham,
" fhall not be abfolved of their fins,
" if they do not firft reverence you,
" and celebrate on you the holy facri-
" fice, which I have commanded to
" my people through the mouth of my
" prophet Mahomet.—Love God—
" pray—give alms."—' After this fer-
' mon, the people falute the mountain
' and depart.'

INDEPENDENT of any argument to be deduced from this account of the pilgrimage to Mecca; the ineftimable value and fovereign importance of it in the conception of the people, and even in the eye of government, would have appeared evident to any one pre-fent at Conftantinople, when a fingular

acci-

accident happened to the caravan returning from Mecca to Damaſcus in the year 1757.

The paſcha of Damaſcus, is generally the conductor of the caravan, or *Emir Hadge:* Ezade Paſchaw had enjoyed that poſt many years; he had ſovereign credit amongſt the Arabs, had married into one of their chief tribes, his poſſeſſions in the neighbourhood of Damaſcus were incredibly extenſive, and his generoſity equalled them; the kiſlar-aga, who was in power the year before, and governed in the ſeraglio, blinded by venality, and not foreſeeing conſequences, removed Ezade Paſchaw to the paſchalyck of Aleppo, and named to that of Damaſcus an obſcure man, on whom he had juſt conferred the three tails; he became of courſe Emir Hadge, or conductor

I

to

to the caravan: his fucceeding Ezade
Pafchaw was crime fufficient in the eyes
of the principal Arabian tribes, but
his refufing them a fmall tribute, the
payment of which had been fufpended
by * Ezade Pafchaw's credit, rendered
them furious and implacable; they
affembled to the number of 40,000,
attacked the caravan, beat the pafchaw
of Sidon, who waited on the road to
fupply it with provifion, flaughtered
numbers of the 100,000 pilgrims
which compofed it, and plundered all
their effects.

* Some time after, the Porte, determined to
remove Ezade Pafchaw from Aleppo to Urfa;
but he was fo beloved by the people of Aleppo,
that they refufed admittance to the new pafchaw,
and ftood on the defenfive.—The Porte paf-
fively fubmitted for the prefent, but however
engaged Ezade Pafchaw next year to accept
the government of Urfa; he was not long
there before the vizir Ragib Pafchaw, by ftrata-
gem, had him feized, and made him atone for
what they called his difobedience with his head.

NEVER

NEVER was confternation greater, among all ranks of people, than on this event; when the fugitive foldiers who guarded the caravan, returned to Damafcus, they fell a facrifice to the citizens fury, as betrayers of the faith; at Conftantinople they looked on their religion as loft, and the gates of falvation fhut up. The depreffion was inconceivably great, and it was univerfal; grief and defpair was vented only in fullen murmurs, no one dared to fpeak out; the fultan was *Ourfus*, Unfortunate: he was fcarce fafe on his throne. The argument in his favour, was, that this mifchief happened in the time * of fultan Ofman his prede-

* On fultan Muftapha's acceffion, the kizlar-aga, who, in fultan Ofman's reign, had removed Ezade Pafchaw from Damafcus, was, for various mifdemeanours, banifhed by the vizir to Rhodes; but on difcovering that his venality and corruption had principally occafioned

ceffor:

ceffor: it excufed the prince, but did not abate the anguifh, or tranquillize the perturbed minds of his fubjects, anxious for the ftate of their fouls. Himfelf, not lefs agitated, conferred continually with the vizir; every precaution was taken to fecure quiet in the capital; but what made his concern the greater, was the lofs of fome facred relicks of the prophet; by the difplay of thefe on the prophet's birthday, he had propofed to augment the devotion, and heighten the folemnity with which that feftival is celebrated.

this deplorable event; the miniftry, glad to exculpate themfelves and appeafe the people, by fixing the odium on fuch an object, fent for his head, which was placed between the Seraglio gates, with a large label on it, expreffing, *That he was a traitor to the faith, and the caufe of that facrilegious attack of the* Arabs *on the* Mecca *caravan.*

THIS

THIS pilgrimage, of such spiritual importance, has been the cause of all the wars between the Persians and the Ottomans; for the latter, who are followers of Omar, think the Persians, or the sect of Aly, unworthy of salvation, and no possible objects of divine favour: they would not therefore, were it in their power to prevent it, permit them to enter Mecca, and defile that sacred way, destined for, and left open to, the truly orthodox only; but the sect of Aly will not tamely suffer the road of Paradise to be thus barred against them. No earthly claim could excite such cruel vengeance, or cause such horrible effusions of blood, as this dispute has occasioned amongst the different sects of Mahomedans.

HENCE it is, that the Persians in all their negociations of peace with the

Otto-

Ottoman Porte, infift on a full and entire liberty for the followers of Aly to go unmolefted on the pilgrimage to Mecca. This important ftipulation makes up almoft the whole of the treaty of 1746 *.

* The emperor of Morocco, with whom the Grand Seignor has fcarce a connexion, and who is almoft unknown at Conftantinople, fent very lately two ambaffadors, with prefents of great value, merely and folely to fecure this pilgrimage to his fubjects.

CHAP. III.

Of Sects.

WHILST there are men, there will be a diversity of opinions and sentiments, especially concerning matters of faith.

THE herd of mankind are, indeed, familiarized with any religion ; the nurse throws in the first ideas, the parent or priest confirms, education rivets it immoveably, it grows with their growth, and becomes inalienable from the man.

BUT this remark, though generally true, is not universally so ; many must and will think for themselves : and of this number, some prompted by enthusiasm and intemperate zeal, others by vanity and a false ambition, will be

led

led to promulge their heterodox conceptions, either on a prefumption of
truth, or the affectation of fingularity,
and of differing in opinion from the
reft of mankind.

It is abfurd for laws to pretend to
bridle thought, or to inflict pains and
penalties on the underftanding; the
more opinions are reftrained, the more
men become obftinate, tenacious,
and determined; contract a defperate
contempt of all laws and government,
and fet them at defiance.

We ought therefore by no means to
be furprifed, when we find a variety
of fects among Mahometans : no religions from the beginning of the world
have been exempt from them. Let them
exift, provided the moral order of fociety is not difturbed; enthufiafm will

fome-

fometimes rage with greater zeal than wife men would wifh, but generally it flames, and at laft extinguifhes like an *ignis fatuus*. Thus, indeed, the Turks feem to think; executions, tortures, pains, and penalties inflicted on account of religion, are never heard of among them.

IF the rituals of the eftablifhed religion are performed, and a convenient conformity obferved, they enquire no farther about it.

* Religious difputes are unknown amongft the Turks. They have not

* Mr. Reland, in the preface to his *Relig. Mabomet.* encourages the ftudy of the Arabian language as a means of converting the Mahometans to the Chriftian religion; by enabling us to demonftrate to them the falfhood and impofture of their own: he acknowledges, that content with their *Koran*, they entrench themfelves fecure from all affaults of arguments, on

the

the art of printing; and I am apt to
think, the difficulty of tranfcribing

the implicit belief of its doftrines, and will not
difpute. That, neverthelefs, they formerly
difputed concerning religion, though in his
own time they could not. He fupports his opinion by quotations from Sollerus, who tells us,
that Raimond Lully had publickly difputed with
Turks in Africa; and from Maracci, who re-
lates, that many miffionaries of the church of
Rome had done it with fuccefs: and what is
more, * Guadagnola informs us, that a Ro-
manift having written a book called *Speculum
verum oftendens*, or, The Mirror of Chriftianity;
Akmed ben Zin Ulabadin anfwered him, under the title of *The Polifher of the Mirror*, &c.
and that Abbé Renaudot, in his Hiftory of the
Patriarchs of Alexandria, has collected from
feveral libraries manufcripts of difputations,
Jews with Turks, Monks with Jews; the Me-
tropolite of Nifibis in Diarbekir with Abuika-
cem; and, ftrange to relate, Abulcoza, or Abu-
caza's Apologetical Conference in favour of the
Chriftian religion, before the calif Almamon,
by Ebnafal, &c.

I fhall only obferve, that the Turks are in-
variable in their manners and cuftoms; whence
in general I muft conclude, that their conduct

* Profeffor of the Arabian language at Rome in the laft
century.

nume-

numerous volumes, and the apprehen-
fion of being betrayed by the tranfcri•

in religious matters remains on the inviolable
plan of their anceftors. They are bred to an
implicit faith in their *Koran*, fo that a very
doubt of its veracity is criminal; this Reland
confefles : but he furely forgot that Raimond
Lully's firft fermon brought on him martyrdom,
at the age of eighty, in Mauritania. The fate
of St. Stephen prevented him from preaching a
fecond time.

He has likewife forgot that the Romifh miffionaries from the beginning, and to this day,
have dealt merely in impofition and pious fraud :
that in the accouhts they fend to the Propaganda
at Rome, they conftantly magnify their own merit and fuccefs, hoping, by that means, to continue in the liberty they enjoy during their miffion; or if that cannot be effected, to obtain
higher eftimation and fuperior employment in
their convents at home, fo as to render that flavery tolerable, which they generally repent of
having fubmitted to, and which they afcribe either to their own childifh inexperience and folly,
or to forcible means employed by their parents
defirous of eafing an overburthened family ; or
elfe to the intrigue and cajollery of fome cunning
monk. All this is evident to any unprejudiced
man who has converfed with them in Turkey.

Lbers,

bers, may be a principal caufe that the reveries of particulars have not been diffufed amongft numbers.

WHATEVER enthufiaftic refinements, or religious whimfies, therefore, feize a Turk, they centre in himfelf, and ferve at moft as mere confidential entertainment to a few friends.

Were the apologies Reland mentions, ever publifhed or promulged to Mahometans? Did not the author of the *Mirror* transform himfelf into the *Polifher?* I dare affirm, if they were not the work of the fame hand, they were of the fame fect; and that thefe Conferences were as unknown among Mahometans, as the authors of them are at prefent to us: and as there is not a miffionary, or Chriftian, who dares now write, or fpeak to a Turk about religion; fo there never was in thofe times of ftill greater barbarifm, any one who could have ventured to do either, without undergoing Lully's fate. Not a fingle inftance can be produced of the converfion of a Mahometan to any other religion, fince the commencement of the Hegira.

THERE

THERE is, however, one sect in Turkey, principally at Salonica, of a very particular kind: it has sprung from one Sabati Sevi, a Jew of the last century, who pretended to inspiration and the Messiahship, and has many followers. They profess publickly the Mahometan religion, and retain privately the Jewish rites, much on the principle of the Ebionites, among the first Christians: they intermarry, inhabit together in the same part of the town, and never mix with Mahometans, except on business and commerce, or in the mosches: they never frequent a synagogue, nor acknowledge their schism. It is difficult to conceive how they remain unnoticed by the Turks; or rather, it shews with how easy a composition the Turks are content in these matters. An outward profession of their own religion compensates for the

private

private exercife of the other; though were thefe Jewifh Mahometans publickly to profefs both, they would be inftantly made a publick example: death is the doom of an apoftate.

WHATEVER other fects the Mahometáns may have among them, they differ merely in words and metaphyfical jargon; and, by what can be difcovered, abound more among the *Sibiites*, or Perfians, than among the *Sunites*, or orthodox Turks. Poffibly, •the clear, light Perfian clime, or moft exalted Perfian language, is better adapted to produce tranfcendant flights of imagination, than the groffer Afiatick, or Thracian clime; or than the mixed Turkifh dialect, compounded, perhaps, of the very dregs of the Perfian and Arabian tongues.

It

It is impoſſible, we are told, to attain in any other language the immenſe ſublime of Perſian poetry ; and, indeed, as far as I could find, almoſt impoſſible for the beſt tranſlator to convert it even into common ſenſe : it ſeems therefore no wonder, ſince they abound with numberleſs poets, raiſed by the higheſt vein of enthuſiaſm, that the ſame ſpirit ſhould lead them into extravagant, enthuſiaſtic, unconfined flights about religion ; and the rather, as they have not the heathen deities to play upon as the ſubject of their ſong.

· But what is certain, there are among the Turks many philoſophical minds. They have the whole ſyſtems of Ariſtotelian and Epicurean philoſophy tranſlated into their own language ; and as they find the latter, which they call the Democratical, cuts more effectually

at

at the root, and is more conformable to their prefent indolence, eafe, and fecurity, they generally adopt it; fo that, perhaps, without their knowing it, they are at once perfect atheifts and profeffed Mahometans.

Superstition and its train are a true bafis for atheifm; there is no medium; from the one extreme the mind is forcibly, tho' imperceptibly, driven to the other: hence the Turks eafily plunge into it; and hence amongft fome nations profeffing Chriftianity, Materialifm is now, with certain ranks of people, the prevailing doctrine.

CHAP.

C H A P. IV.

Of Mahommedan church-government, ~~and their civil~~

CHURCH government in Turkey, notwithſtanding the miſtakes authors have committed on that ſubjeſt, ſeems not to be involved in much intricacy. At the inſtitution of Mahommedaniſm, it appears, as if it had centered in the *Mufti*, and the order of *Moulahs*, out of which he muſt be choſen. It is difficult to ſay what ſhare they have in it at preſent; they ſeem, however, to be conſidered by moſt as eccleſiaſtics, and the *Mufti* as their head; although they are generally and really regarded by the Turks rather as chiefs of the law and expounders of it; and this, indeed, is their viſible and moſt known office: ſo that whatever

may

may have been the original inftitution of the order of *Moulahs*, if they were at firft merely churchmen or divines, I think they muft be confidered as partaking little of that charaƈter at prefent.

Those who really aƈt as divines are the *Imaums*, or parifh-priefts, who pofitively officiate in, and are fet afide for, the mere fervice of the mofches. * Their *Scheiks* are the chiefs of their *Dervifhes*, or monks, and form religious communities, or orders, eftablifhed on folemn vows : they confecrate themfelves merely to religious

---

* The *Scheiks* frequently preach with virulence and inveƈtive againft government ; thence, or from the refpeƈt for religion, real or affeƈted, they are mightily careffed and reverenced by the greateft men in office : the vizirs have generally a favourite one about them, who often behaves with uncommon freedom and impudence.

offices,

offices, domeftic devotion, and publick prayer and preaching: there are
four of thefe orders, the *Bektafhi, Mevelevi, Kadri,* and *Seyah* *, who are
very numerous throughout the empire.

* It may, perhaps, be proper to infert fome
account of thefe four orders of Mahometan
monks.

1. The *Bektafhi* were founded by one Hagi
Bektafh, whofe fepulchre is now in a village
called Beficktafh, on the European fide of the
Bofphorus, near Galata; the Turks pay it
great refpect and veneration.

Thefe monks, according to their inftitution,
may marry. They are chiefly met with in
country towns or villages, and are obliged to
travel through the empire; they muft give the
Gazel and *Efma* to all the Muffulmen they meet,
and to them only. The *Gazel* is an affecting
tone of voice, which they apply in a fpecial
fenfe to the Divine love. The *Efma* is the in-
vocation of one of the names of God, of which
the Turks have among them one thoufand and
one.

2. The *Mevelevi* take their name from their
founder Mevelana. Thefe turn round in acts
of devotion with fuch velocity for two or three
hours fucceffively, that not even a trace of their

No church-revenues, as far as I could learn, are appropriated to the

countenance is perceivable by a by-ftander. Mufic is their delight, particularly a flute made of an Indian reed; they live in their monaftery, profefs poverty and humility, appear exceeding modeft and kind to ftrangers, receive all thofe of any religion who come to vifit them, and accept alms. They treat ftrangers of any nation with coffee; and if a Muffulman's feet, or fandals, fhould be dirty, they offer immediately to wafh them. They have a convent in Pera.

3. The *Kadri* are a fingular order, whofe inftitute and devotion confifts in maccrating their bodies; their looks are diftracted and irregular; they walk the ftreets almoft naked, rarely covering the thighs; they hold their hands joined together, as if at prayer, except when they dance, which religious exercife they will continue many hours, and fometimes the whole day, repeating inceffantly with uncommon vehemence, *Hu! Hu! Hu! Hu!* one of their names of the Deity, until at laft, as if they were in violent rage or phrenfy, they fall to the ground foaming at the mouth, and bathed with fweat from every part of the body. This order was once abolifhed, but is fince revived. They

parti-

particular ufe of the *Moulahs:* the *Imaums* are the ecclefiaftics in immediate pay.

have a convent between Pera and St. Demetry, and receive all thofe who go to fee them.

4. The *Seyah* are like the Indian *Fakirs*, meer vagabonds ; they have monafteries ; but when once they are out of them, they feldom return. They obtain eafily a leave of abfence from their fuperior, on condition of fending a certain quantity of provifions or money to the convent. They are, indeed, infolent fturdy beggars, who will not be refufed. When they enter a town or a village, either in the public praying or market-place ; they ftand up, and cry moft vehemently, *Good God ! fend me a thoufand dollars ! or, a thoufand meafures of rice !* &c. The people then flock about them, giving alms ; and when they find they have exhaufted the charity of the place, they march on to another town, and repeat the fame practice, until they have collected the fum impofed on them by the fuperior of their convent.

In general, thefe itinerant monks are a fet of determined villains and thieves, have influence only on the low fuperftitious part of the vulgar, on which confideration chiefly, it fhould feem, they are countenanced by the Turks of

Mecca

Mecca and Medina abforb large
fums. The repairing and beautifying
their mofcheès, fupplying their lamps
with oil, and furnifhing numberlefs
implements for their ufe; paying many
lay dependants who attend that fervice;
fupporting the *Mechtz*, *Medreffes*, or
publick fchools; the *Immarets*, or hof-
pitals for the fick, incurable, or mad;
are the other means by which the re-
mainder of that vaft and enormous in-
come is expended.

Most writers on the Mahometan
religion, extracting their knowledge
from Arabian authors of the very
early ages of the *Hegira*, have, I

fafhion, who, though they think them no effential part of the Mahometan inftitute, ca-
refs and encourage the fuperiors of this order,
or fuch amongft them whofe pretenfion to more
eminent fanctity has gained an afcendence over
the minds of the common people.

E   think,

think, too pofitively blended and confounded it with their prefent law: not confidering the changes which time produced in the Mahommedan fyftem; for the *Koran* containing political inftitutes as well as religious dogmas, was probably fufficient to regulate the civil affairs of Mahommed's firft followers, a few Arabians, as remarkable for their poverty and the fimplicity of their manners, as for their courage and enthufiafm; and the immediate fucceffors of thefe men, poffeffed with a religious veneration for this production of their prophet, continued to blend together in the fame perfon, the functions of the prieft and that of the judge; and thus perplexed for a time religious with civil rights.

But when his followers became numerous, and their dominion was fpread over

over many opulent and extenſive
regions, not only religious orders
ſprung up, to eaſe the Hierarch of what
he thought the drudgery of his office;
but alſo law-digeſters aroſe, who now
finding the doctrines of the *Koran* inſuffi-
cient for the great end of government,
viz. the preſerving of good order, and
the well-being of civil ſociety, have re-
medied its defects without appearing to
derogate from its authority, or riſquing
to alienate the leaſt part of that implicit
obedience, and profound veneration,
the people paid to it; for under pretence of forming commentaries, as a
ſimple extenſion of the angel's or the
prophet's ideas, they have provided
codes of civil law, equal and ſimilar
to the code, pandect, or digeſt; as clear
and copious as *Cujas* and *Domat.*

Abou

Abou Hanife is one of the first and chief of those who have thus commented on the *Koran :* his books, and those of his disciples, are the rule of law under the Turkish government in Europe and Asia.

In this manner the original institutes were augmented, so far as related to civil and criminal cases ; indeed it certainly must have been necessary to form new regulations, when conquest, riches, and luxury, had introduced new crimes, and new subjects of contention. And thus, it should seem, the ecclesiastical and the civil first became, in some measure, distinct and separate departments ; the *Moulahs, Mufti*'s, &c. presiding in the courts of justice, and the *Imaums,* &c. officiating in the moschees; though still the exact boundaries of each jurisdiction are hardly to be defined.

The

The ingenious prefident Montef-
quieu *, led by precarious authorities,
has excluded all right to the poffef-
fion of private property; all right to
fucceffions; all inheritances in families,
or to females and wives; and, indeed,
all † civil law from among the Turks.
In fhort, he feems to think, that the
Grand Seignor's defpotifm fwallows up
the whole code of right in that empire.

When I fee the excellent reafoning,
and the many judicious confequences
deduced from fuch erroneous principles, by fo acute and penetrating a
genius; I cannot help thinking it a
ferious inftance, how fubject we are to
error, and how fallacious the moft plaufible arguments may fometimes prove.

* L'Efprit des Lois, lib. v. cap. xiv. & xv.
† L'Efprit des Lois, lib. vi. c. 1.

With-

WITHOUT appealing to fact, the
single chapter intitled * *Women*, would
have shewn him how successions in families, and to male, or female, or
wives, are fixed and regulated by the
prophet; and consequently, how far
private property is secured by law beyond the reach, and out of the power,
of the sultan.

THE other part required but a single enquiry; he might easily have
been informed by what method they
actually determine causes in their courts
of justice, and what † books they use

* Chap. IV. in Sale's Edition.

† *Extract out of a Law-Book used in the* Turkish
Courts, by Hanife. [Chap. of Sales.]

Sales are made when the one consents and the
other accepts, explaining himself by the pre-
terit of the Indicative Mood; now when any
one of the contracting parties consents to sell,
or to buy, the other shall be at liberty to ac-

in

in Turkey as authorities for their le-
gal decifions: he would have found

cept, or not, as long as they remain in the
place where the bargain is to be made.

But if the one confents, and the other goes out
from that place before accepting, the bargain
is void.

The fale is concluded when both pofitively
agree; then neither the one nor the other can
be off, except fome fault or defect fhould be
found in the thing fold, or that the buyer had
not feen it.

It is not neceffary to know the quantity of
goods expofed to fale, in order to bargain for
the whole; for though a price is fpecified, the
fale is not valid until the quantity and quality
are known.

Sales may be for ready money, or on credit,
fixing the time of payment; and when the fpecies in which the goods are to be paid for is
not fpecified, it is to be underftood the moft
current money of the country; but if there
are different fpecies of current-money, the fale
is not valid without fixing the particular
fpecie.

All eatables may be fold, and all forts of
grain by the eftablifhed *meafure*, or without it;
either by taking a vafe or tub of any kind, the
exact contents of which are unknown; or by

feve-

feveral, which formally ftipulate, and fix, the terms and legality of a pur-

weight, taking a ftone for a weight, the real weight of which is unknown.

Selling a quantity of any eatables at a drachm the *Cafiz*, the fale fhall be valid for one *Cafiz*, according to the opinion of Abu Hanife: but when the feller declares how many *Cafiz* there are, or may be, then according to his two difciples the whole is fold.

He that fells a flock of fheep, at a drachm a fheep, the fale will not hold for the whole flock.

In like manner for a piece of ftuff, or filk, at a drachm the ell, he muft mention the number of fheep or ells.

If a quantity of eatables of a hundred *Cafiz* are fold at a hundred drachms, and there are found lefs; the buyer will be at liberty to take them in paying only for what there is, or he may refufe the whole: but if there are more than an hundred meafures, or *Cafiz*, he muft reftore the furplus to the feller.

But he that buys a piece of ftuff, or filk, on the footing of ten ells at ten drachms, or, one hundred cubits of land at a hundred drachms; if lefs is found, he is at liberty to take them for the faid fum, or to leave them; if there are more than what is agreed for, they

chafe,

chafe, whether of lands, houfes, corn, cattle, or merchandize. From thefe it may be prefumed, he would have

belong to him, and the feller has no right to the furplus.—But if the feller declares that the land contains a hundred cubits, and that the price is a hundred drachms, or a drachm the cubit; in that cafe, if there are more or lefs, the buyer is at liberty to take it at a drachm the cubit, or to leave it.

If a bale of filks or ftuffs, faid to contain fifty pieces, is fold at fifty afper-, or at one afper the piece, and that there fhould be found fewer pieces; the buyer may take what the bale contains at an afper the piece, or he may refufe the whole; but if there are more than fifty pieces, the bargain is void.

When a houfe is fold, all the buildings belonging to it are included in the bargain, tho' not exprefly mentioned; or on the fale of a piece of ground, the palm, or other trees ftanding in it fhall be included, though not mentioned; but the herbs, or other greens, growing in it are not comprehended.

If the palm, or other trees are fold with the fruit on them, the fruit will belong to the feller, unlefs they are fpecified in the bargain; but then the buyer can oblige him to gather the fruit immediately.

ac-

acquired a notion of Turkifh defpotifm very different from that which he has adopted.

THE *Moulahs,* however, whether confidered as churchmen or lawyers, enjoy great immunities, which defcend uninterruptedly to their families. Their lives and eftates are generally fecure; their greateft punifhment in office, even for malverfation, is exile; and if they are not too obnoxious to government, they may fometimes compound for that by a pecuniary donation. All the profitable employments of the law are in their hands; they are fent out as *Mufti*'s, or judges, throughout the chief towns of the empire, whence they are pro-

---

If fruit is fold on the tree, whether it proves good or bad, the bargain is valid, and the buyer muft gather them immediately.

moted

moted to the high office of *Cadilef-
quier*, or chief juftice, either of *Rome-
lia*, or of *Anatolia*; that is, of Europe,
or of Afia; and at laft to that of *Sheik
Iſlam*, or *Mufti*, at Conftantinople.

CHAP.

CHAP. V.

Of the Koran.

I SHALL not pretend to enter into a minute analyfis of the feveral doctrines of the *Koran*, but confine myfelf to fome general obfervations.

MR. SALE has given us an elaborate detail of that book, in the preliminary difcourfe to his excellent tranflation. I am, however, forry to fay, that he frequently difcovers an inclination to apologize for it; and rather endeavours to reconcile and palliate the numerous abfurdities he meets with, than to expofe them in the light they deferve. One advantage, however, we derive from this humour of his, we may be certain he has not added an abfurdity to thofe he found, nor given

any

any of them a more ridiculous drefs than they wear in the original.

Some heterodox manufacturers of wit, defirous of appearing fingular, tho' at the expence of common fenfe, if not of common honefty, have not fcrupled to profefs themfelves admirers of the *Koran*, have extolled its doctrines, and dared even to put them on a parallel with thofe eftablifhed by our facred writings.

Mahomet, fuperior to his countrymen in parts and fcience, refolved to be fupreme in command. To effect this he had but one game to play, which was to impofe himfelf on them as a prophet divinely infpired, and his book as an immediate revelation from the Almighty. In this he could inculcate what doctrines,

7   and

and affign himfelf what pre-eminence
and authority he pleafed : in fhort, his
book was of the utmoft confequence
to him. He therefore, very artfully,
framed it after the prototypes of truth,
the Mofaic and Chriftian revelations;
for in his travels to Egypt, as well as
at home among the Chriftians and Jews
in Arabia, fugitives on account of religion, he muft have obferved the force
with which thefe genuine revelations
had captivated the minds of men; he
therefore, without impugning either,
declares the latter of them to be only
a continuation of the former, and
that his own is a continuation of both,
and compleats the whole difpenfation
of Divine Providence. This he has
judicioufly feafoned with what he knew
would render it moft acceptable to his
countrymen, and appears moft predominant in himfelf, the indulgence of

their

their luft and rapine in this world, and a moft fenfual paradife in the next.

His firft ftep was to perfuade his ignorant Arabians, that the *Koran* is an extract taken from the great book, in which, at the creation of the world, the Divine decrees were all written and depofited at the fame time in one of the fub-firmamental heavens; and that from thence it was faithfully delivered to him, verfe by verfe, by the chief hierarchical angel Gabriel. Hence, in his chapter *Al Kadr*, he tells them himfelf, from the mouth of the Almighty, " Verily, we fent down the *Koran* in " the night of *Al Kadr*; and what fhall " make thee underftand how excellent " the night of *Al Kadr* is? The night " of *Al Kadr* is better than a thoufand " months: therein do the angels de- " fcend, and the fpirit Gabriel alfo, by " permiffion of their Lord, with his de-

" crees

" crees concerning every matter. It is
" peace until the viſiting of the moth*." .

On this paſſage principally, is founded the claim of the *Koran* to be of ce-
leſtial origin, the all-beauteous and all-
perfect work of the Creator; and hence
that moſt profound veneration, amount-
ing almoſt to adoration, which the Mahometans pay to it. They fancy a chapter or verſe can cure them of all diſ-
eaſes, preſerve them from all accidents,
or external evils; can prolong life,
and render it healthful and proſperous.
A thorough ablution is neceſſary before
they preſume to touch this ſacred book;
the ſight of an infidel pollutes it; and
when they read they muſt hold it above
their middle, to preſerve it from approaching the region of impurity and
defilement.

* Sale's Edit. Of Divine Decrees, ch. xcvii.

to

THE Turks are eternally puzzled when, or which night, this *Al Kadr* may be: they think it muft be in *Ramadan*; and many enthufiafts have, at that time, extatic communications with the angelic fpirits who defcend from the heavenly fpheres.

MAHOMET, though fo abfolute and fo able an impoftor, did not, however, dare pretend to that great criterion of Divine truth, miracles, the main bafis of thofe true revelations he would endeavour to imitate, and which he confefles to have been wrought * in attefta-tion of their Divine origin. Many urged him to produce them; many afked of him figns; and he feems in many parts of the *Koran*, more embarraffed to evade the charge of impoftor, incurred by not manifefting his

* Sal. Edit. ch. v. 27.

voca-

'vocation by thefe figns, than to efta-
blifh his doctrines. His own uncle
and relations feemed, on that account,
to deteft his impofition ; and it is evident from the text, that he had often
found his very women rebellious ; it
is probable they likewife expected miracles : for he tells us, there were only
four of them good and obedient.

WHEN he is preffed for this proof
of his miffion, he fhifts the want of
it on the will of the Deity ; " * They
" (the Infidels) have fworn, fays he, by
" God, by the moft folemn oath, that
" if a fign come unto them they would
" certainly believe therein : verily, figns
" are in the power of God alone, and
" he permitteth you not to underftand,
" that when they come, they (the Infi-
" dels) will not believe ; and we will turn

* Ch. vi. entitled Cattle, p. 110. Sal. Edit.

" afide

" aside their hearts and their sight from
" the truth, as they believed not
" therein the first time ; and we will
" leave them to wander in their error."
He then recommends them to believe implicitly in the *Koran*.

On another occasion he uses the same
dexterity. " * The infidels say, unless
" a sign be sent down unto him (to
" Mahomet) from his Lord, we will
" not believe. The Lord's answer ;
" Thou art commissioned *to be a preach-*
" *er only,* and not a *worker of miracles ;*
" and unto every people *hath a director*
" *been appointed.* God knoweth what
" every female beareth in her womb,
" and what the wombs want or exceed
" of their due time or number of
" young." The conclusion of this
paragraph is curious ; it is a short turn,

* Ch. xiii. entit. Thunder, p. 201.

F 2   upon

upon wombs, which leaves the beginning upon miracles quite out of fight.

By thefe quotations we may perceive
what evidence his external figns of Divine miffion carried with them; and
as to the internal, they are fo far from
recommending it, that the moft of his
doctrines and precepts, thofe properly
his own, are trivial and unworthy the
flighteft attention. The precepts and
commands copied from the Mofaic
difpenfation, of which there are many,
or thofe from the Chriftian, may command fome regard; although thofe
from the latter favour of the corrupt
channel they have paffed through; for
if he preaches the duties of benevolence,
and the forgivenefs of injuries, it is
not with that univerfal, beneficent, diffufed principle, recommended in the
gofpels indifcriminately to all mankind:
he

he confines thefe virtues undoubtedly
to the narrow limits of his own fect;
for they are neither to live nor com-
mune with unbelievers; and fo far from
being enjoined to forgive them, they
are commanded to injure and to fubdue
them: and God knows, it is but too
evidently fhewn by their practice how
much they honour the precept.

It is, indeed, a pleafant part of the
Koran, which reprefents the Divine
communications defcending fo low as
to regulate the minuter interefts, family concerns, and amorous paffions
of Mahomet; it muft give us a pretty
juft notion both of the prophet and
his people, as well as of thofe fceptics
who have expreffed fo favourable an
opinion of his book: for inftance, let
us hear the awful commands of the
Almighty impofed on the prophet's
rebellious wives, &c. on fo important

an

an occafion as the vexatious demand
they made for fine clothes: to fatisfy
this demand was a difficulty, perhaps,
too arduous for the power of man
alone to overcome.

- " * O Prophet, fay unto thy wives,
" If ye feek the prefent life and the
" *pomp thereof,* come, I will make a
" handfome provifion for you, and I
" will difmifs you with an honourable
" difmiffion ; but if you feek God,
" and his apoftle, and the life to come,
" verily, God hath prepared for fuch
" of you as work righteoufnefs a great
" reward. O wives of the prophet,
" whofoever of you fhall commit a ma-
" nifeft wickednefs, the punifhment
" thereof fhall be doubled unto her
" two-fold ; and this is eafy with
" God : but whofoever of you fhall be
" obedient unto God and his apoftle,

* Koran, ch. xxxiii. p. 345, 356. Sal. Ed.

6   " and

" and shall do what is right, he will
" give her her reward twice, and we
" have prepared for her an honour-
" able provision in *Paradise*. O wives
" of the Prophet, ye are not as other
" women ; if ye fear God, be not
" too complaifant in fpeech, left he
" fhould covet, in whofe heart is a dif-
" eafe of incontinence.—Sit ftill in your
" houfes, and fet not yourfelves forth
" with the oftentation of the former
" time of ignorance. Obferve the ap-
" pointed time of prayer, give alms
" —and obey God and his apoftle ;
" for God defireth only to remove
" from you the abominations of va-
" nity, &c.

TERMAGANT and rebellious wives
were the leaft punifhment that a man of
the prophet's infatiable paffion deferved;
inftead of four, a number he allowed
his followers, and furely fufficient to

F 4   break

break the eafe, and deftroy the happinefs, of any one man living, he again
brings down the Deity to grant him a
permiffion without limitation, and even
to direct his amours. If he had been
fmothered under them all, it would
have been a juft death for fuch extravagant lubricity. *Satia te fanguine,*
was the faying of the Scythian queen,
when fhe plunged Cyrus's head into
a yeffel of blood.—But let us hear
again his Lord.

" * O Prophet, we have allowed
" thee thy wives, unto whom thou
" haft given their dower ; and alfo the
" flaves which thy right-hand poffef-
" feth, of the booty which God hath
" granted thee ; and the daughters of
" thy uncle, and the daughters of thy
" aunts, both on thy father's fide,

* Koran, ch. xxxiii. Sal. Edit. p. 348, 349.

" and

" and on thy mother's fide, who have
" fled with thee from *Mecca*; and any
" other believing woman if fhe give
" herfelf unto the prophet, in cafe the
" prophet defireth to take her to wife.
" This is a peculiar privilege *granted*
" unto thee above the reft of the true
" believers: we know what we have
" ordained them concerning their
" wives, and the flaves whom their
" right hands poffefs, left it fhould be
" deemed a crime in thee *to make ufe*
" *of the privilege granted thee*; for God
" is gracious and merciful. Thou
" mayft poftpone the *turn of fuch of*
" *thy wives as thou fhalt pleafe*, in *being*
" *called to thy bed*; and thou mayft
" take unto thee her whom thou fhalt
" pleafe, and her whom thou fhalt
" defire, of thofe whom thou fhalt
" have before rejected, and it fhall be
" no crime in thee: this will be more

2 " eafy,

" eafy, that they *may be intirely content*,
" and may not be grieved, but may
" be well pleafed with what thou fhalt
" give every one of them.——O true
" believers, enter not the houfe of the
" prophet, unlefs it be permitted you
" to eat meat with him, without wait-
" ing his convenient time.—And when
" ye afk of the prophet's wives what
" ye may have occafion for, afk *it* of
" them from behind a curtain; this
" will be more pure for your hearts
" and their hearts. Neither is it fit
" for you to give any uneafinefs to the
" apoftle of God, or to marry his
" wives after him for ever; for this
" would be a grievous thing in the
" fight of God."

MAHOMET's paradife flowing with
delicious waters, planted with the moft
odoriferous trees and fhrubs; but above

all,

all, the exalted enjoyment of black-eyed nymphs, would lead me farther than I intend.

THE few quotations exhibited here, merely to fave a reader the trouble of recurring to the *Koran* itfelf, may fuf-ficiently evince what marks of fanctity, and of a divine miffion, we muft ex-pect from it: they will likewife de-monftrate, what a moft abject idea the prophet, and his ignorant followers, muft have had of the Divine perfec-tions; and what grofs contradictions paffages like thefe muft be, to thofe pompous and fublime defciptions of them, with which they are moft impi-oufly mixt. I fhall follow Mahomet no farther in his lubricity, but fay with the prophet Habakkuk, " he that runs " may read."

I MUST however obferve, that fome
of his laws, if not rigidly juft, are yet
an effectual fecurity againft defpotifm,
and the oppreffion of the people, efpecially fuch as relate to private property, widows, orphans, inheritances,
legacies, and crimes, &c.

ONE conclufion I think fo clear, that
it muft be evident to all fagacious and
impartial men; it is, that the whole
Koran is a difcordant, incoherent jumble
of fentences, gleaned from fugitive Jews
and Chriftian fectaries, Neftorians, Mo-
nothelites and Eutychians; ftrangely
put together by the prophet, and impofed on ignorant enthufiaftic people,
who muft have been great barbarians
when they believed it the word of
God.

WE

WE poffefs many good tranflations of this extraordinary book, made from genuine and ftandard originals : excellent ones were found among the Granadine Moors by cardinal Ximenes, and correct copies may always be purchafed in Turkey; tho' at a high rate. Indeed, there is fcarce a rifque or poffibility of being impofed on; for the Mahometans hold it as the higheft facrilege to alter a fingle point or jota of this their facred book : and moft men of letters amongft them, like the Jews in Paleftine, think it not only a duty, but a fpecial recommendation to the Deity and his prophet, to have every word and tittle of the *Koran* fo fixed and imprinted in their memories, that they may on any occafion repeat it ex- tempore.

DU RYER's

Du Ryer's French verſion may err in the idiom, but the general doctrines are ſufficiently exact; Marracci's Latin one is very correct; and that in Engliſh by Mr. Sale, is undoubtedly, in every reſpect, of approved accuracy.

Talking on this ſubject with a learned *Effendi,* who was known to have the *Koran* by heart; a chapter from Sale's edition was explained to him in the vulgar Turkiſh dialect: the old Turk, in a ſort of rapturous ſurpriſe, followed the interpreter; repeating verſe by verſe in the original Arabian. He remained aſtoniſhed and amazed; and aſked with ſome emotion, how we could have ſo perfect a tranſlation, the ſenſe ſo juſtly preſerved? and added, that the author muſt have been an admirable proficient in the Arabian language, a very great man.

I CAN-

I CANNOT conclude this chapter without obferving, that from what I have faid of the practical religion of the Mahometans, we are not to infer that they are univerfally, and without ex-ception, deftitute of virtue; nor of all humanity towards ftrangers. I have already, in my general character of the Turks, anticipated this remark as far as I could confiftent with truth. I could not help, however, repeating it, bad as they are, they are the beft peo-ple in their empire.

THAT corrupt religion perverts the rectitude of nature, that the Turks are notoriously corrupted by it, is too true; but how many ignorant abfurd fects of Chriftians are there, who, each deviating from the original inftitutes and pure precepts of Chriftianity, are ftrangers to that perfect fimplicity and uni-

univerſal benevolence it requires; and are as deſtitute of ſocial virtue and common humanity towards thoſe who differ from them in opinion, as the moſt zealous or ignorant Turk?

CHAP.

C H A P. VI.

Of Despotism, and its Restraints.

MEN, either from habit and the prejudices of education, or from presumption and opinion, are apt to think their own government the best; to censure others, point out their defects, and frequently, without sufficient knowledge to judge, will venture to revile and abuse them.

THE government of the Turkish empire has been injuriously misrepresented by censurers of this kind. The tremendous accounts given of its despotism have misled many, and raised the religious passions of some to abhorrence and utter detestation; while others, not under the influence of religious passions, have found their nature

G   shocked

shocked at the image these accounts
conveyed to them : and well regulated
as the system of this haughty court
may be, both have been brought to
annex the idea of barbarism to it; have
supposed it without order or plan, entirely subject to the caprice, cruelty,
and avarice of a tyrant, tending merely to the oppression of his subjects, and,
as far as its power extended, to the
destruction of mankind.

SURELY these men did not, or would
not, look nearer home : it was, perhaps,
too near; for let us only cast our eyes
about us, and impartially examine the
governments with which we are sur-
rounded, we may then perhaps find,
that the Sultan is not more despotic than
many Christian sovereigns; perhaps,
not so much as some of them.

AL-

ALTHOUGH it is abfurd to look for perfection in any body of laws, or any political inftitutions ; fince the productions of the human mind, limited as it is, muft all be imperfect ; yet the moft equitable conclufion will be, that in every empire which has extended wide, and flourifhed long, there are fome parts of its conftitution wife and good : and it is certain, that whatever defects may be in the political fyftem of the Turks, their empire is fo folidly founded on the bafis of religion, combined with law, and fo firmly cemented by general enthufiafm, and the intereft, as well as vanity, of the Turkifh individual, that it has lafted ages, and bids fair for ftability and permanency.

WE have feen in a former chapter, that the Turks have laws to fecure property and regulate commerce ; they

have

have others to punish crimes and restrain vice. It is not their laws, but
the corrupt administration of them,
the flagitious venality of their judges,
and the number of false witnesses con-
nived at, and whose testimony is accept-
ed, that is the opprobrium of the
Turkish empire, as will be more fully
shewn in a succeeding chapter.

How far Mahomet intended to li-
mit, or extend the power of the sovereign, I shall not pretend to determine;
the degree in which the present sultans
are absolute, is an enquiry more to the
purpose. Of this, facts will best enable us to judge: those we shall produce will shew us the nature of the
Turkish monarch's despotism; and that,
independent of fear, the constant com-
panion and restraint of tyrants, he is
limited by religion and law. But we

2   shall

shall first confider the right of his claim to inherit the poffeffions of fome of his fubjects.

THOSE who are directly employed in his fervice, and thofe lefs immediately fo; for example, the officers under *Pafchaws* in diftant provinces, know that they hold their offices on a kind of feudal tenure : they, notwithftanding, eagerly follicit, and contentedly accept them on that condition; fubmitting, or, it may be faid, covenanting and agreeing, that he fhould inherit at their death.

THE affinity of this law or cuftom with the tenures of the old feudal law, transferred, in this inftance, from lands to office, would lead us to think it had its origin from thofe tenures; for they prevailed over almoft all the

known

known world, at the time the *Koran* was formed; and they fubfifted a-mongft ourfelves long after the Con-queft.

By thefe tenures, lands held in fief reverted, on the death of the holder, ab-folutely and irrevocably to the feudal prince, or lord: the family were left to fcramble the wide world for fubfift-ence; they had no claim of recovery, nor even a pretenfion to relief in their neceffities, except from mere commife-ration and humanity.

MAHOMET, either by chance or defign, has effectually fecured the peo-ple from the immediate inconvenience and oppreffion of that tenure.

ESTATES, in land or houfes, annex-ed to the church, either in actual pof-

6   feffion,

feffion, or in reverfion, are held both
by prince and people facred and inviolable : thofe perfons therefore, by
whatever means they acquire their poffeffions, who give the reverfion to religious foundations, tranfmit them unmo-
leftedly and unalienably to their direct
male iffue : Mecca and Medina are the
places generally preferred, becaufe
held the moft facred.

THEY call this fettlement *Vacuf:*
they pay an annual, very trifling, quit-
rent, until the extinction of that iffue,
when the whole devolves to the religious foundation on which it is fettled.

THIS previous law, or tie of religion, binds the prince to fo rigid an
obfervance, that there has never been
a fingle example of even an attempt
to trefpafs or reverfe it.

FOR,

FOR, independent of what he may conceive his duty towards God, or his prophet, the leaſt breach of ſuch a law deſtroys the very foundation of his throne : it is merely by the *Koran*, or their religious inſtitutes, his ſovereignty exiſts ; the moment he abandons thoſe doctrines, or violates thoſe laws, he becomes an infidel, and ceaſes to be the lawful ſovereign.

MAHOMET has not limited this law of ſecurity merely to his own ſectaries ; it extends to all religions ; Chriſtians or Jews may avail themſelves of it ; and as moſt of them, led by ambition or intereſt, aſpire to enjoy more or leſs the countenance and favour of the great officers in government, they generally take the advantage of that protection to ſettle their poſſeſſions either with Mecca or Medina ; or, perhaps, with

greater

greater facility, fome one of the feveral mofchees at Conftantinople, or where-ever elfe their fancy or connexions may lead them; it is enough that it be a religious foundation.

THE Jews, indeed, have been excluded fome mofchees, as it appeared by the regifters, that in the fpace of a hundred years, not a fingle reverfion fell in; whence the Turks, it fhould feem, have concluded, that the direct male iffue of the fons of Abraham is eternal.

FROM what has been faid of the *Vacuf*, it is obvious, and it is worth obferving, what immenfe revenues belong to the church; and how in fucceffion of time it muft fwallow up into its enormous bofom, almoft all the lands and poffeffions of that vaft empire.

CHAP.

CHAP. VII.

Facts to elucidate the foregoing chapter, and of the Turkish government.

THE Grand Seignor is confidered as abfolute fovereign of the whole Turkifh empire; the fubjects approaching him treat him as a divinity, with the higheft veneration and refpect. He fhould, ftrictly adhering to their conftitution, delegate his abfolute power to the Vizir. This was practifed by moft of them from Mahomet the IId's time to 1730.

THE rebellion that year, the depofition of fultan Achmet, and the acceffion of his nephew Machmut, gave a new turn to the conftitution. There was, at that time, in the feraglio, where

he

he generally acts as first minister, a *Kiſlar-Aga*, or chief of the black eunuchs, an experienced and wise man: he had been in office under Machmut's father, predeceſſor to the depoſed Achmet; he had ſeen two rebellions, two depoſitions of the ſovereign, obſerved the cauſe, traced the evil, and pointed out the remedy.

THE cauſe he aſcribed to the permanent continuance and abſolute power of the Vizirs; to their ambition of glory, and reſtleſs diſpoſition for war and conqueſt. He therefore counſelled the new Sultan to retain the power in his own hands; to change his Vizirs frequently, not ſuffering any one to continue in office above three years, and to live in peace with all his neighbours. On theſe maxims he adviſed his maſter to eſtabliſh the tranquility

of

of government, and the fecurity of the
throne; and fultan Machmut, during
a reign of twenty-four years, fteadily
adhered to them.

THIS black eunuch lived to the age of
ninety; he died in 1746, and was fucceeded by his favourite *Bekir-Aga*, a young
Black, about thirty-three years of age,
born in the ifland of Borneo. Full of
fpirit and vigour, he found himfelf, by
the policy of his late mafter, in poffeffion of abfolute power, and haften-
ed to exert it; but he wanted the wifdom, the judgment, the knowledge of
mankind, and experience his predecef-
for poffeffed; his will became his law,
and he fet no bounds to his avarice.

INTOXICATED with higher ideas than
his underftanding could fupport, he
laid down as a maxim, That no man in
                                    the

the empire fhould be worth above
10,000 * dollars, and acted as if he
would not leave them an afper.

THE rage of his paffion was for
diamonds, jewel-work, and rich toys;
probably, indeed, to lay in a ftock of
portable wealth for an evil day, and to
live in fplendor at Cairo, the ufual
place of their exile. During the fix
years of his adminiftration, one would
have thought that he intended to exhauft
all Europe of diamonds, and purchafe
the whole produce of the mines of
Golconda and Brazil.

THE inftruments of his extortion
were, a young flave of twenty-two or
twenty-three years old, and an Armenian raifed from the duft. The go-

* A dollar makes 120 afpers, and is worth
two fhillings and fixpence.

vernment of that vaft empire centered in the hands of this junto. When any large purchafe of diamonds was to be made, the means were concerted between thefe three how to raife the money: they fagacioufly divided the neceffary fum into parts; they then applied to a number of opulent great men, who were, or had been in office; and giving them to underftand it was to purchafe prefents intended for the fovereign, they affigned a part on each until they had compleated the whole fum. No one dared repine, nor even hefitate; fome were filent through fear; others, perhaps, moft of them, from the expectation of future favours.

THIS rapine was varioufly talked of; fome afcribed it to the prince, fome to the Black and his affociates; the more general voice gave it to the former,

mer, who certainly could not be entirely ignorant of the extortions practised by his minister. They occasioned, however, no commotions or disturbances.

HIGHLY in the Sultan's confidence and favour, he might, indeed, have gone on with these and other irregularities without controul ; but his first successes spirited him on to enormous acts of power against all decency, law, and religion ; he not only meddled with those dependent, but even with independent people. He injudiciously offended the body of Janissaries, by stopping the pay of some, and withholding the money which had been promised them for rebuilding their *Odda*'s, or chambers, lately burned down ; and at last, he struck against those whom he had feared most, the men of the law.

AN

An important caufe was depending before the *Moulah*, or judge of Scutari, a man of fingular refolution. The party who was in the wrong applied to the Black and his creatures for protection, and backed their requeft with a large prefent. The junto undertook it, and fent a meffage to the judge, that he fhould decide the caufe in favour of their friend: he anfwered, that he would pronounce according to law, and his own confcience; and on various like follicitations, he as conftantly perfifted in the fame anfwer.

The day he was on the bench to hear, and finally determine the caufe, a * *Chiohadar* of the Black's entered the court-room with precipitation, and heard the fentence pronounced againft their friend. He abufed and threatened

* Head fervant.

the

the *Moulah*, drew out a fhort whip they generally wear, and fome pretend, went fo far as not only to fhake and menace, but to ftrike.

THIS unprecedented infult on law and religion, ftirred up the *Moulah* to feek redrefs and revenge: he applied to the *Mufti*, who fent him to the Vizir. That minifter fought, by all poffible methods, to pacify him : every offer was rejected, even that of the *Moula-lick* of Iconium, the beft in the empire. The men of the law fupported their brother, and murmured filently, but deeply. What heightened their indignation was, that whilft the Vizir capitulated with the *Moulah*, the Black rewarded his *Chiohadar* with a lucrative meffage abroad.

H

THE Black and his dependants perceived the storm arifing; they found they could not filence the *Moulah*, and therefore determined his deftruction. This could not be done openly; yet their Arabian craft, blinded by rage, paffion, and defpair, did not enable them to concert it with their ufual diabolical fubtlety, or to perpetrate their villany with that fecrecy the evil they expofed themfelves to required.

THE bungling project they hit upon was to fend ruffians in the dead of night, who ftrangled the *Moulah* and his daughter in their beds: in the mean time, they cut the wooden pillars fupporting the houfe, and fo demolifhed it, that it might appear as if they were accidentally buried under the ruins.

THE time, method, and circumftances, led to a clear difcovery of all this.

this horrid tranfaction. The men of the law became defperately refolved on vengeance, and joined fecretly with fome chiefs of the Janizaries; but determined to fpare the fovereign, provided he gave up his Black, the obnoxious *Kiflar-Aga.*

THE difficulty lay how to make their firft grievances known to him: if through the black eunuch, the natural channel, any two or three complainants rifked fudden deftruction, without effecting what they defired; if fecretly to the Sultan, they were not fure of a better fate. They found, therefore, only one method which might effectually awaken, intimidate, and inform him; that was, by burning of Conftantinople.

FIRES

FIRES continued inceffantly for near twenty days, every day in two or three different parts of that city. The Grand Seignor finding the evil deep, and carried on by defign, depofed the Vizir; a facrifice he imagined would appeafe the rage of difcontent: but he found that expedient was infufficient; for the next day as many fires appeared. At the laft he was advifed, as it was faid by fome, to confult fecretly the *Mufti*; or, as others report, that chief of the law went to him fpontaneoufly, and boldly laid the whole iniquitous conduct of the Black before him, demanded juftice, and told him, he expofed the fecurity of his own throne in refufing it; urged the neceffity of taking fome immediate determined party againft the Black; adding, if the Sultan would not give *Bechir* the *Kiflar-Aga* up, he defired leave to refign

his

his own office, that he might rather as a private man fee the dreaded cataftrophe of his prince's fall, than as the head of the law be conftrained to confent to it.

SURE it is, that the *Mufti* was really a man of that ftoical felf-denying turn, that heroic mind, as to dare hold fuch language, and undertake this harfh and hazardous meffage to his fove- reign, who immediately gave attention to this alarming remonftrance, deter- mined to get rid of the Black, and to exile him to Cairo.

ON one of his ufual days of recrea- tion, the Sultan went by water to a *Chiofk*, or fummer-houfe, on the Bof- phorus: the *Boftangi-Pafhi*, and *Seli- chatar Aga*, who always accompany him, had already received his orders. The Black was of the party; they feized

on

on him at his landing, forced him into a boat, and imprifoned him in Leander's tower*, where he was to wait for the galley defigned to tranfport him to Cairo.

THE fight of the galley excited frefh remonftrances from the Law; they demanded the delinquent's blood, and obliged the Grand Seignor, though with the utmoft reluctance, to confent to his execution.

THE high fpirit of the Black was changed to defperation at the fight of the executioner; he refolutely defended himfelf with his *Hanjar*, or knife, againft that officer: he wounded him; and fell at laft but by the fuperiority of the fcimitar: his body lay expofed three days on the fea-fhore.

* Situated on an ifland, in the port of Conftantinople.

DAILY

DAILY executions followed of all his creatures and dependants, his flave, his Armenian, and his fecretaries; many others were exiled.

THE fums confifcated by death and exile were immenfe. What paffed thro' the *Tefterdarat*, or public treafury, and was afterwards paid into the Grand Seignor's *Chafne*, or private treafury, collected from without, amounted to 30,500 purfes, or a million nine hundred thoufand pounds fterling. What was found within the Seraglio in diamonds, jewel-work, and gold, was never known; but in general affured to be as much more, or far exceeding it.

THIS moft rare and remarkable fact in their hiftory, and which fo immediately and intimately affected abfolute power, might fingly fhew how law at

laft

laſt can effectually controul it, and
bring the ſovereign, as it was well
known in this caſe, againſt every ſentiment of love and affection, and almoſt without a precedent or example,
to abandon the governor of his Seraglio, and at that time of his empire, to
the utmoſt rigour of the juſtice of law.

But that even the Sultan thinks himſelf bound by law, is evident from his
practice; for, on any treaty to be
made, any war to be undertaken, or
tranſgreſſions puniſhed that are committed againſt himſelf, or by perſons of
high rank in his ſervice; he applies to
the *Mufti* for his *Fetfa*, his decree, his
deciſion, or ſanction of law.

It is true, as he makes the *Mufti*,
he can depoſe and exile him, the worſt
that can happen to him. It is alſo as

true,

true, that many of them, in different reigns, have actually withstood the will of their Sultan; and that, notwithstanding, he has not dared immediately to resent their non-compliance. On these occasions it has been judged neceffary to invent some more plausible pretence for disgracing them: the argument against violent proceedings, would, in this case, be too clamorous with the people; those of the law alone might shake his throne.

THE *Koran*, we have observed, secures property; and the following remarkable instance will confirm the practice.

IN the year 1755, the * Porte was burnt entirely down: on rebuilding it

* The Porte is the palace in which the Vizir resides: in it all the archives are kept, and all public business transacted.

the

the confideration was, how to place it
on the former fpot, and at the fame
time render the fituation fecure from
a like accident for the future.

THE method determined on, was,
to leave a fufficient void fpace about
it, and for that end to purchafe and
demolifh feveral houfes that were con-
tiguous. Moft owners fubmitted to a
fale; but there was one old woman who
declared fhe could not, and would not,
part with hers; that it had been a property in her family for feveral genera-
tions, and no money could compenfate
the infinite value it was of to her: no
offer tempted her, no threats could
avail. The men in power cried out
and abufed her; but the injuftice appeared too violent to dare take it by
force; the houfe ftood; and when it
was afked why the Sultan did not ufe

his

his authority? take it, and pay the value? the anfwer was, *'Tis impoffible, it
cannot be done, it is her property.*

NOTWITHSTANDING the tranfcendant expreffions the Turks ufe when
fpeaking of their Sovereign, they will
frequently murmur, talk freely, abufe
him and his minifters, throw anony-
mous fcurrilous papers into the mofchees,
and feem ever ripe for rebellion, if out-
raged by frequent and unufual oppreffion and tyranny. They are taught
that he is eftablifhed by God, that he
is a defcendent of their prophet, thro'
whofe mediation they expect falvation;
and yet in a moment they will deprive
him of his throne, of his liberty, and
even of his life.

THIS may appear only a fingle inftance of the immenfe number of feem-

ing

ing contradictions in the compofition
of human nature : though, indeed,
were it fo, it might with other fuch
inftances be accounted for, by what a
fagacious * free writer has attempted
to prove, that men do not generally
act according to principles.

ALTHOUGH I think his propofition
too general, it is, I fear, in great part
true ; for, that there are many men
who do not act according to principle,
is but too evident : this might therefore, in appearance, furnifh a folution ;
but here would be mifapplied and infufficient; for the whole of what Turks
are taught relating to government, is
not taken into the cafe ; and therefore
the fact is not fairly reprefented.

FOR they learn very early, that if the
prince is of right divine, he founds it

* Bayle.

on the *Koran*; that he is conftituted ſuch by that ſacred code of laws; which as a true believer he has ftudied, and knew, before his acceſſion to the throne, it would ever be his duty to obſerve; and that, conſequently, he is as much bound and tied by all thoſe laws, as they themſelves are.

This is ſo explicitly and fully laid down in the *Koran*, that Mahomet thought it neceſſary to throw in rules of exception exprefly for himſelf.

Hence when the people are notoriouſly aggrieved; their property, or that of the church, repeatedly violated; when the prince will riot in blood, or carry on an unſuccefsful war; they appeal *to Law*, pronounce him an infidel, a tyrant, unjuſt, incapable to govern; and, in conſequence, depoſe and impriſon, or deſtroy him.

They,

THEY, it is true, confult firſt their own power, or the probability of ſuccefs, rather than the rectitude of the action, but always under the ſanction of the law, directed by ſome one of the legiſlature ; and it may be affirmed, that no example will be found of the depoſition of a Sultan in Turky, but a form of law, either true or falſe, has been obſerved : nay, it ſeems abſolutely neceſſary ; for it has always been practiſed, that either the *Mufti*, or * the *Nakib of Santa Sophia*, or of *Eiup*, or at leaſt, ſome diſtinguiſhed man of the law, ſhould enter the Seraglio, or tent, and even declare the reaſons of the depoſition to the very Sultan ; announcing to him why by law he is unworthy and incapable of reigning.

* Head, or director of the moſchees, who are emirs or deſcendents of Mahomet.

FEAR

FEAR obliges the Turks to paſſive obedience, merely as diſunited individuals: then they only talk;—but when once the burthen of ills accumulate and extend, they find a chief; the law and ſoldiery join with the people as in a common intereſt, and depoſe the oppreſſor; but always place on the throne his lawful ſucceſſor.

THIS ſingle undoubted practice of taking the *lawful Succeſſor* proves they ſeek the ſanction of *law*; and I muſt obſerve what perhaps is undoubtedly true, wherever it has not been mere uſurped temporary power, the like has been practiſed in all governments.

CHAP.

CHAP. VIII.

History of the Vizir Ragib Mehemet Pa-
shaw's government.

THE death of the chief Black gave a sudden change to the interior of the Turkish government, and may be considered as a new æra in their constitution. This circumstance, however, is little known, and less noticed : what therefore succeeded, and the advantages taken from that event by the Vizir, to establish his own absolute power, may be worth relating.

THE new *Kislar-Aga*, intimidated by the tragical end of his predecessor, conducted himself with great caution ; he seemed to consult frequently with the Vizir, and enter into closer connexions with him : this continued until the year 1754.

7   BUT

It was then that, on the demise of Sultan Machmut, his brother Ofman afcended the throne. This prince, according to the maxims of Turkifh policy, had been continually confined; and now came forth new into the world at the age of fifty-fix, a perfect ftranger to mankind. On this event, the Black *Kiflar-Aga* began to affume more power, and with his party, compofed of fome without, and fome within the Seraglio, to make and depofe Vizirs as they pleafed. His power within the Seraglio is entirely free from controul, except from his fecretary the *Jazigi Effendi*, who generally gains credit with the Grand Seignor: in thefe two, and a few of their adherents, the whole power of government centered.

On the death of Ofman, in the year 1757, the Vizir Mehemet Ragib Paf-

I   cha,

cha, who had the feals, happened to be the ableft, and moft fubtle man of the Turkifh empire. His office led him to place Sultan Muftapha on the throne: he had either formed a fecret connexion with that prince before, or captivated his affection then, by his obfequioufnefs, learning, and eloquence; fo that he became at once his friend and confidant, and fet the office of Vizir on its ancient footing of abfolute minifter with abfolute power.

THE Sultan, to attach this minifter more effectually to his perfon, obliged him to repudiate an amiable young lady his wife, and to marry the princefs his fifter; a widow, whofe perfon, and advanced years, rendered her an object incapable of exciting the tender paffions.

MUSTA-

Mustapha, the present Sultan, of whom we are now speaking, is a son of Achmet, who was depofed in 1730. The two brothers Machmut and Ofman, who had reigned from the time of that depofition till the acceffion of Muftapha, were defcendants of Achmet's brother.

Filial duty operates with great force on Mahometans; they commonly, I might fay invariably, make a point of imitating their fathers; and quote the life and actions of their progenitors as the only models they ought to follow.

This prince, therefore, looked on all and every regulation introduced fince his father's depofition, or which deviated from the practice of his anceftors, as infufferable innovations; and the reigns of his two coufins appeared to him full of abufes and irregularities.

THE Vizir took care to confirm him in thefe ideas, and to point out the abufes; exclaiming againft them as deviations not only from the practice of his father, but from the ancient Mahometan rule or canon of government: he carried him up to the time of Solyman I. by fome called the Magnificent, by them the Lawgiver; and did not fail to reprefent the power given to the *Kiflar-Aga*, a wild, ignorant black flave, as the fource of thofe and all other attendant evils; that the authority ufurped within the Seraglio, and the iniquitous intrigues always forming there, deftroyed the wifeft meafures of the Porte; and that the true original eftablifhment of the empire, was the abfolute power of the Vizir.

THE Black who fucceeded *Bekir-Aga* ftill continued in power. On feveral occafions casions he had shewn himself no friend to the Vizir, who, nevertheless, had supported himself, during the few months he governed in Sultan Ofman's reign, by means of the *Jazigi Effendi*; he found himself, however, continually tottering, and called himself publickly, a stranger who must prepare to remove. Turks never forgive: the Vizir's ability and art were therefore immediately employed to satisfy his revenge, by punishing this enemy. The Black was condemned to exile; and on the fatal disaster of the Mecca caravan, his head was struck off, and brought to Conftantinople, as a compensation he owed to the people for being the original cause of that sacrilege.

THE power of ministers in this, as in many other countries, is in proportion to the emoluments of their office,

and

and the confequent riches and number of their dependants.

The *Harem*, or ladies of the Seraglio, have a vaft revenue affigned them for their fupport and maintenance: this confifts in large diftricts of lands, and confiderable towns, in Europe and Afia, and is called the *Haremai*. The abfolute independent government and direction of thefe revenues, which amount to thofe of a kingdom, were intirely in the difpofition of the black *Kiflar-Aga*. He received the whole, accountable to no one; in all affairs relating to the *Haremai*, he held the Divans, diftributed juftice; caufes, criminal and civil, came before him; he named the governors, and all the other magiftrates, civil and military; no one dared contradict him, or interfere with him in the government of thofe places allotted

4   lotted

lotted for the maintenance of the *Harem.*

THE difficulty was how to eradicate this part of the conftitution; but Ragib Mehemet Pafcha's refources never failed him: his knowledge of their hiftory, his fertile genius and eloquence, had captivated the Grand Seignor, who was foon perfuaded that this power of the Black Eunuch over the *Haremai,* was the fource of his crimes; that government fhould be more fimple; and that even the bufinefs of the *Haremai* fhould, as a principal and effential part, be annexed to the Vizir's office: in fhort, he got it intirely out of the hands of the Seraglio, and brought it into his own; fubftituting a Black of his own choice, whom he rendered fubfervient to all his views; fo that one might truly fay, he re-modelled that

I 4   part

part of government, and brought the whole empire under his own abſolute power.

I COULD not help often comparing this Vizir's art of governing, with that of Tiberius. In cunning, deceit, and jealouſy, he exceeded him; and where he found a competitor, or one who might endanger his own ſecurity, his cruelty perhaps was not leſs.

A *Tefterdar*, or high-treaſurer, a man of unbounded generoſity, and uncommon ſublimity of ſentiment, occupied that poſt for the ſecond time while Ragib was Vizir, and had gained vaſt popularity. The Vizir heard him continually praiſed: this was a ſufficient reaſon to excite his jealouſy. He ordered a reviſion of accounts; found him, as he pretended, deficient; and procured his exile; at the ſame time

time complaining of the lofs he fuf-
tained by the *Tefterdar*'s removal. Nor
did the Vizir's hatred ftop here; it followed him in his exile, and was not
appeafed but by his blood: he had his
head cut off, protefting all the while
againft fuch cruel juftice, crying and
lamenting as for his friend's hard fate;
cenfuring the Grand Seignor's rigour
and too inflexible feverity, exercifed
on fo able and amiable a man, for a
crime fo common, and for which an
atonement was fo eafily made.

WITH all his credit and power, he
never in the leaft attempted to conteft
the Grand Seignor's will. Subfervient
to it, he advanced to the high and important poft of *Mufti*, one *Veli Effendi*,
a bold loquacious man, much refpected
in the law. This man was not long in
his poft, before he was obferved to
med-

meddle in politics, and was thought
to vie in power with the Vizir.

The Vizir, who had taken an affection to the interpreter of the Porte,
refolved to make a change of princes,
or *Vaywodes*, in Moldavia and Walachia; and to confer one of thofe
dignities on the interpreter. The Sultan agreed to it; the interpreter was
nominated to this promotion; and the
honours to be conferred on him on that
occafion were prepared : but the *Mufti*,
who patronized another, a depofed
prince, came between, and mentioned
him to the Grand Seignor as the pro-
pereft perfon; heightening his com-
mendation with uncommon praifes.

The Sultan mentioned this recommendation to the Vizir; that minifter
immediately confirmed it, and fubmitted to alter his whole plan.

THE

THE interpreter was laid aside, and the *Mufti* had the satisfaction to find his recommendation effectual.

THE Vizir's usual Turkish Proverb was, that " you must hunt the hare in a cart :" that is, Do your business covertly, and avoid precipitation. He received the new prince as if this promotion was his own act, and the new prince his own creature : all went on, seemingly, in perfect harmony with the *Mufti*, for near three months. At length a rumour was industriously spread round the town, as if the *Mufti* had taken one hundred purses of money for his recommendation ; but if this did not reach the Grand Seignor, it failed in its intended effect : the point was how to convey it to him.

THIS

THIS prince, as is cuſtomary in Turkey, frequently went about incognito, diſguiſed as a common man; and introduced himſelf into coffee-houſes to hear what the people ſaid of himſelf and his miniſters.

IT was to one of thoſe houſes in * *Eiup*, that he more particularly reſorted: here the Vizir ſet ſome of his people, and inſtructed them in the language, which, on the Sultan's entrance, they ſhould hold in his hearing. One of them began with ſaying, "they were bleſt with the wiſeſt, juſteſt, and beſt of princes, and wiſhed that his miniſters reſembled him; but what could they hope, when the chief of their religion and law was ſo venal and infamous as to be corrupted by infi-

* A ſuburb near his ſummer palace.

dels?

dels? that the *Mufti* had received a hundred purfes of money to raife a miferable infidel to the dignity of prince of Walachia; and if fuch abominations were fuffered, and that the Grand Seignor fhould not be informed of them, the empire would foon fall into ruin and deftruction." The whole company joined in the accufation: the Grand Seignor alarmed, flipt out, went to the Vizir, and ordered him to depofe the *Mufti* immediately.

THE Vizir expoftulated; he told his majefty, that fuch reports fhould be received with diffidence; that people were often mifinformed, and always difpofed to be cenforious and impertinent; that this report was certainly not to be trufted; that the *Mufti* was too holy, too virtuous a man to be guilty of fuch wickednefs;

6

and

and conjured him, at leaſt, to ſuſpend his indignation until he could more truly and preciſely verify the faСt.

His exhortations and intreaties pacified the monarch for the preſent, until the ſubtle miniſter poſted a new group in another Coffee-houſe, to repeat the accuſation, with additional aggravations againſt the *Mufti*. The firſt was then confirmed beyond a doubt; the prince would no longer ſuffer a delay, but ordered the *Mufti* into immediate baniſhment, to a moſt diſagreeable ſituation at Synope on the Black Sea.

The Vizir appeared to all his friends under the utmoſt concern at this event. The *Mufti* applied to him with moſt fervent entreaties, to have the place of

ba-

banifhment changed, and that his departure might not be fo inftantaneous:
the minifter reprefented the difficulty
of prevailing with an irritated, paffion-
ate, juft prince. However, he promifed to ufe all his intereft to mitigate the fentence, and that he would, as
effectually as poffible, implore his majefty's clemency.

He fuffered the *Mufti* to remain a
day or two at a country-houfe on the
Bofphorus; and afterwards obtained
for him, what this difgraced man and
his friends fo ardently defired, the place
of his banifhment to be changed from
Synope to Brufia.

Thus after giving him a fatal blow,
he yet referved to himfelf the merit of
having moft effentially ferved him.

CHAP.

C H A P. IX.

Change of Vizirs.—Order of Bufinefs.—
Policy of Turk Minifters.

THE change of Vizirs, and fometimes, though rarely, their execution, has brought on a general prejudice, and been produced as an argument of the inftability and diforder
of the Turkifh government: Sultan
Machmut, as I have obferved, introduced that change as a maxim of ftate,
and was the firft who methodically
practifed it.

SOME who were of the very loweft
clafs of men, feveral of whom could not
write or read, have occupied that high
office; yet the order of government,
and the clue of bufinefs, has not
been a moment interrupted. Another
maxim.

maxim more certain and falutary pre-
ferves government in its equal regular
courfe; for fubalterns in office are religioufly continued, and generally on
changes advanced: fo that thofe who
are many years trained and practifed
in the bufinefs, become the Vizir's
amanuenfes and inftructors. Hence,
any new Vizir is foon mafter of the
modes of government; or if he is
not, as to the moft difficult and intri-
cate parts, he is fo far at leaft as to
keep the empire and the capital city
in quiet, the men of the law in good
humour, and to mafter the foldiery;
the which, perhaps, are the chief and
moft important ends of his great power.
By this proceeding of government, no
mutation of the higher officers ever
affects the whole; fo that when we read
of a * *Chiaia* to the Vizir, a † *Reis Ef-*

---

* Second in power to the Vizir.
† Secretary of State.

K

fendi,

fendi, a * *Chiaous Paschy*, depofed, the
fpirit of the office remains, and the bufinefs ftill goes on in its proper courfe.

THE clerks and under-clerks are almoft innumerable. Some hundreds of
hands are kept conftantly at work at
the Porte, and each of them with the
leaft talents or genius afpire to fome
of the higheft dignities; keep their
eye immediately fixed for years on
the office they hope to fill; and by
an obftinate perfeverance, and never
moving out of that courfe, they frequently attain their end.

THERE is no Chriftian power can
vie with the Porte, for care and exact-
nefs in their feveral offices: bufinefs is
done with the greateft accuracy: in
any important writing words are weigh-

* Marfhal of the Court.

ed,

ed, and that fignification conftantly
taken, which may moft conduce to their
own advantage.

PAPERS of the remoteft date, if
fingly the year of the tranfaction is
known, may be found at the Porte;
every command granted at that time,
and every regulation then made, can be
immediately produced.

THE rule which government follows
in the explanation of treaties, or capitulations, or conceffions granted to
Chriftian princes, or in many other
cafes, is *Precedent*; the remoter the
example, the more refpectable; and
moft fo, what they call the *Ancient Canon:* any political fuit in doubt, or
depending between themfelves and the
Chriftian Powers, may be immediately
determined by producing Precedent.

THE

THE French ambaſſadors have often pretended ſuperiority of rank at the Porte: the Turks have as ſolemnly declared to others the nullity of their pretenſions, and that all ambaſſadors are on the ſame footing. But as the publick audiences are by rotation, ſome one muſt begin, and be the firſt: hence they take the prime occupant, the firſt ambaſſador who was eſtabliſhed in their country; and this is the ſingle reaſon why the French have the priority in point of time at audiences, but they have none of order or pre-eminence.

WHEN they have a mind to expedite buſineſs at the Porte, or that it is agreeable to them, no people do it with a greater celerity; when the contrary, they will as artfully protract or delay: numberleſs excuſes, good and

bad,

bad, are ready; it may remain fufpended for months or years.

THE idol the Turks worfhip is gold; and in all common affairs their ears are opened by that powerful deity. If that is not made ufe of, the claim of right, engagements, capitulations, or treaties, have often and generally no effect; fome mafter hand muft feel the weight of this fpecious golden argument: but then they are often generous enough to truft to a conditional promife, and are content with the fee after the completion of the bufinefs.

THE policy of every Turkifh minifter has himfelf for its firft object; they ftudy folely their own fecurity and permanency in office: this is the only fyftem they are to be taken with. It is in vain to talk of the intereft of

the

the empire, either prefent or future; the queftion to themfelves is, Can I be fafe? Can I hold power? If therefore matters of high confequence, of peace or war, are propounded to them; if the one or the other does not coincide, perfectly, with the prefervation of their own power, and efpecially their perfonal fafety, all the money in the univerfe will not move them.

SOME time after the acceffion of Sultan Ofman to the throne, the Vizir who had handed him to it, found his credit fallen with that prince; that others had the royal confidence, and were plotting and intriguing his depofition.

EDUCATED in the Seraglio, he was no ftranger to its intrigues, and affiduoufly endeavoured to counterwork his

his enemies; but the mines he had laid were generally sprung against himself; so that he found his ruin inevitable.

The *Reis Effendi* under him was a haughty stern Muſſulman; the name of a Chriſtian ſeemed adverſe to his very nature; and every paſſion was excited, if the leaſt miſunderſtanding aroſe between the Porte and any of the neighbouring powers.

The Vizir, in full vigour of age, thought he could make a proper uſe of this zealous ſecretary of ſtate, whoſe fiery temper, he ſaw, might readily be prompted to plunge the Porte into a war, and war he ardently wiſhed for: it ſeemed the moſt effectual means by which he might preſerve himſelf, augment his ſway of power, and, at the

K 4   head

head of an army, command even the
Grand Seignor, and effectually crush
his own enemies.

THERE had been trivial disputes
and bickerings with a neighbouring
Christian court, and some serious altercations; but the Sultan's temper, disposition, or political maxims, had led him rather to pass over
than to resent them.

THE disputes were known to the
Vizir; he found them proper materials
to work on the innate hatred the *Reis
Effendi* bore to Christians, and the contempt in which he held them; and
give him a welcome occasion to declare
his ardent zeal for the honour and
glory of Mussulmanism and the Sultan. To this man therefore he opened
this contentious affair, loading it with

every

every aggravating circumftance; yet, feigning to foften the fury of his paf- fion, though he knew it was rather the moft effectual means to excite it, he thus brought him to become his ftalking-horfe in the Seraglio; fet them all in a rage, not excepting the Sultan himfelf; and brought them from threats and menaces almoft to action.

THE Vizir prepared to put himfelf at the head of the army, to attack that power by whom they were, as the Grand Seignor and *Reis Effendi* pre- tended, fo fcandaloufly and ignomini- oufly infulted.

THE junto who managed this great affair at the Porte, confifted of five perfons: the zealous fecretary of ftate always took the lead; the Vizir, fubmif- five to the will of the fovereign, fimply

ap-

approved; though when commands
were made out for the troops to af-
femble, he expreffed himfelf to his
confidants with the greateft fatisfaction
and joy.

But, at length, one of the junto
opened the fcene to a foreign minifter,
to whom the negotiation had been entrufted; told him the eafy means by
which the Grand Seignor and *Reis
Effendi* would be fatisfied, the Vizir
difappointed, and the empire preferved
in peace.

That foreign minifter made a proper ufe of it; ftopped for the moment,
at the rifque of his own life or fafety,
the precipitancy and fury with which
they were carrying on their revenge;
and as what they required was more
honourable for the other court to grant,
than for them to accept, the whole af-

fair

fair was adjusted with almost a single word. The Vizir was soon after depofed and exiled.

Thus ended a violent, precipitate, turbulent negotiation, which lasted a considerable time; entirely set on foot by one man's lust of power, who, to secure that, and his dignity, or to perpetrate his revenge on a few, would have been the cause, perhaps, of the destruction of his country, but certainly of many thousands of his fellow-creatures and fellow-subjects.

This personal policy has frequently manifested itself in lesser matters. Their distant governors often aspire to independency, and obtain it. At Babylon, Achmet enjoyed this usurped plenitude of power for several years; and what is more extraordinary, his son succeeded him,

him, with undiminifhed authority, un-
difturbed by the Vizir, and died a natural death in his government. Not
long after, his fon-in-law Solyman Pafchaw poffeffed himfelf of the fame
poft, and maintained the fame indepen-
dence. They difregarded the Sultan's
commands; and though they always
anfwered in terms of refpect and fubmiffion, they always acted according
to their own will. The Vizirs chofe
rather tamely to fubmit to this infolent
treatment, than by refenting it to excite
rebellion or rifk their own fecurity, and
therefore contented themfelves with
their mere external profeffions of obedience.

ANOTHER remote governor has fupported himfelf on the fame footing
for many years; but as he is worfe
circumftanced, and not fo thoroughly
fecure, he muft therefore feek fome
un-

underhand protection in the Seraglio, or at the Porte.

On the death of the Chief Black and his adherents, that protection was loft; he applied at Conftantinople to fecure in his intereft a *Reis Effendi* of fordid venality: for this purpofe he furnifhed a credit for a confiderable fum, and, moreover, promifed twenty-four of the fineft Arabian horfes for the Vizir and his minifter. The perfon entrufted fent one to found the *Reis Effendi*; for fuch meffages are always grateful. On his return, he reported that he left him hefitating, but difpofed to accept: it was then thought proper to tempt him with a part of the bribe. The meffenger was again difpatched to him with a large bag, fealed. The *Effendi* took the money, put it into his bofom, mufed, rubbed his head,

ftroked

ſtroked his beard; but at length, drawing the meſſenger cloſe to him, told him in a whiſper, he was obliged to him and his principal for intermeddling: he knew that taking the money from them was ſafe; but from the other, the governor who ſought protection, it might be dangerous to himſelf, he could not truſt him: he then returned the bag, adding, that ſuch a ſtep required much reflection. He never would receive the money; ſo that the governor was obliged to ſeek other protection; and muſt have found it; for he exiſts ſtill with his uſual independency.

END of the FIRST VOLUME.

OBSERVATIONS

ON THE RELIGION,

LAW, GOVERNMENT,

AND MANNERS,

OF THE TURKS.

VOL. II.

LONDON,

Printed for J. NOURSE, Bookseller to His MAJESTY.

MDCCLXVIII.

CONTENTS.

ERRATA.

Page 64. line 12, *for* Regib, *read* Ragib.

Page 98. line 15. *Instead of*—walking abroad an airing on foot, *read,* walk abroad, and take an airing on foot.

OBSERVATIONS, &c.

CHAP. X.

Adminiſtration of Turkiſh Juſtice.

THE monarch's deſpotiſm is not the greateſt evil in Turkey : his ſubjeĉts would perhaps bear that without much murmuring, or great diſtreſs. The radical deſtruĉtion of all ſecurity lies in the iniquitous adminiſtration of their laws, which are an impending ſword in the hand of corruption, ever ready to cut off their lives and properties.

THE overflowings of a tender mind muſt not lead us to conclude that the steady conduct of the *Moulah*, or judge of Scutari, and his positive refusal to comply with the *Kiflar-Aga's* command, arose from his inviolable attachment to strict justice; for from the general and known practice it is rather to be inferred, that this *Moulah* was secured, pre-engaged, and pre-determined, by the potent motive of a bribe; and that thus tied down, he did not dare act otherwise, nor even venture to obey the peremptory command of the Black Eunuch.

THEY tell us of some rare examples in Turkey of uncorrupt judges; I have heard of one, but I have known none.

THERE are in Conftantinople several courts where caufes are determined, and the plaintiff may choofe in which to prefer his suit. The inferior are, the *Moulah* of Galata, and the *Stambole Effendi*, or judge of Conſtantinople; the higher, the two *Cadi-leſquiers*, or judges of Europe and Aſia; and laſtly, the Vizir's divan, which is the ſupreme court of judicature.

MAHOMET has exempted his deſcendants from the authority of theſe juriſdictions; they are numerous throughout the empire, and are always judged by the heads of their tribe: in any cauſe, therefore, in which an *Emir*, or * *Green-head*, is concerned, their proper court is that of the *Nakib* of Sancta Sophia, or *Eiup*; though I have obſerved the Vizir always keeps a watchful eye over them, and occaſionally controuls their proceedings.

* The deſcendants of Mahomet are called Green-heads, from a green turban they wear.

THE

THE plaintiff has not only a confiderable, but almoſt a certain advantage over the defendant ; for as he chuſes his judge, his firſt care is to ſecure him.

ALL the judges have a *Naib*, or deputy, who is the real acting man, and generally guides and determines the maſter : to this man the firſt application is made, and the bribe is offered : if he finds the ſum worth while, and accepts, you are for the moſt part ſecure of gaining your ſuit.

SOMETIMES, by bribing higher, the defendant may nonſuit his adverſary ; or he may at leaſt, by quirk and quibble, be enabled to poſtpone the cauſe ; perhaps, to remove it to another court ; and thus protracting it, if he is the richeſt, tire him out, until, at length, the

the plaintiff is obliged to drop his pretenſions, juſt or unjuſt, and content
himſelf with accepting a trifling com-
poſition.

THE means of ſpinning out a ſuit,
and eluding a deciſion, are various; a
defeᴄt in the forms of procedure, ab-
ſence or death of witneſſes, denying
the validity of ſeals, the hand-writing
of others, or even their own; or, as
ail proof is determined by witneſſes,
and that theſe are found in abundance
who will ſwear any thing for pay, when
a cauſe is deſperate, an immediate reſource is at hand; for ſuch witneſſes
may be brought to any point as will
puzzle the cleareſt cauſe, and juſtify
the law's delay.

THERE are different ſpecies of witneſſes; ſome your neighbours and old

ac-

acquaintance; others, cafual; and laftly,
thofe who make a profeffed trade of
attending courts of judicature, and
live by it. On informing them of the
merits of the caufe, they firft declare
that they appear in it merely becaufe
they fee the hardfhip and injuftice intended againft you; that, as they
know you to be an honeft man, on
whofe veracity they can abfolutely de-
pend, they will therefore affirm as
truth whatever you fhall aver to them
as fuch. This profeffion, which they
make with an affected earneftnefs, is
the ufual Turkifh falvo, and feldom fails
to appeafe all their qualms, as well as
quiet all their fcruples.

Or fhould it not have that effect;
if the witneffes infift on better information, they are concealed in a private
place, where they can hear all that
paffes

paſſes in an adjoining apartment. Into this apartment the party with whom you are at variance is decoyed, and there ſuch conceſſions, by interrogatories, and other artful managements, are drawn from him as may make againſt himſelf: theſe the evidences report on the trial, and declare they have heard. Often indeed, on this occaſion, inſtead of the real party, a friend of your own, who perſonates him, is introduced into the apartment, where he makes what conceſſions you pleaſe in the hearing of the concealed witneſſes, who can neither ſee nor be ſeen, and who do not chuſe to detect the fraud, but report to the judge what they heard, as ſpoken by the real perſon. In law-ſuits, no practice of this kind can ſtartle a Turk; all he is anxious for, is ſome pretext, which he thinks may enable him ſtill to paſs for

an.

an honeſt man. Thus much for their firſt ſpecies of witneſs.

THE laſt ſort are thoſe who make a profeſſed trade of it, and are always ready at any man's ſervice for a dollar or two. By habit and long practice theſe need no caſuiſtry, no ſalvo to their conſcience, but ſwallow their oath, true or falſe, and will ſtand or fall by their evidence.

THE judges have their deputies, who manage their retainers, and other dependants; fellows who conſtantly attend the courts to bring them cuſtom: their buſineſs is to foment litigation, or to raiſe falſe ſuits, called *Avanias,* and attack thoſe on any pretence who are rich and can pay. No man is ſecure from day to day, eſpecially if he be a Chriſtian or Jew; for let the

cauſe

-caufe on which the procefs is founded, be ever fo improbable, abfurd, or falfe, he muft appear to it and defend it, when, if he has not fecured the judge, a cloud of witneffes are brought in, by whofe teftimony he is affuredly caft.

Many inftances daily happen of demands on property, or complaints of injuries committed, which never had, and never could have, the leaft grounds of exiftence.

In general, let the caufe be right or wrong, Chriftians or Jews have no chance againft Turks but by dint of money; happy, if that can fave them.

Neither Chriftians nor Jews are admitted as evidence againft a Turk; but Chriftians or Jews can witnefs for or againft each other.

THEY

THEY have no fubpœnas; the law does not permit a fummons, or oblige any perfon to give in their evidence; they muft do it uncompelled. Turks, unlefs your dependants, will not appear in favour of Chriftian or Jew: the mere force of money muft bring them into court. If they really know the juftice of the caufe, and have feen the fact, they generally expect the higher bribe; and that in proportion as they think their evidence material. If it is for a Chriftian againft a Turk, it is fcarce poffible at any rate to engage them.

A GREEK built a houfe, and planted a large garden on a piece of ground which had been poffeffed by his family near fourfcore years : all the *Hoggets*, or deeds of conveyance, were in his hands, paffed in due form of law by the original

ginal Turkiſh proprietor from whom
it was purchaſed. He nevertheleſs
found himſelf ſuddenly attacked with a
law-ſuit by a grandſon of that Turk,
who declared that his grandfather had
not ſold the ground; that as his father
and he had been long abſent on the
Grand Seignor's ſervice in the Perſian
war, they could not lay in their claim
before; but that he had now the witneſſes to prove that the Greek's deeds
of conveyance were abſolutely falſe,
and therefore inſiſted to be put in poſ-
ſeſſion of his ground.

THE only reſource the Greek had
left was, to remove his ſuit from an
inferior court, to which he was ſum-
moned, to the Vizir's divan, which,
as he was under foreign protection, he
eaſily obtained. His intention by that
ſtep was not to bring it to a hearing;

he

he knew that the witnesses against him
were ready, and that he would inevit-
ably lose his cause; but the use he
made of it, was to bribe some considerable officers of the Porte, to threaten
and deter his adversary; whilst underhand he had others who were bring-
ing him to a composition, by which
means he stopped all farther prosecu-
tion, though at no inconsiderable expence.

THESE cases happen daily to Christians and Jews; especially such as the
Turks suspect, or know, to be opulent;
often amongst the Turks themselves,
but with more caution, as they can
out-witness each other with more facility, and that generally the rich can
eat up the poorer. Hence may appear, how precarious purchases of
lands or houses made by Christians
or

or Jews are in Turkey; yet it is their ruling paffion to poffefs both.

A MAIN defence or proof in any depending caufe, is a *Fetfa*, the previous opinion or decifion of the *Mufti*. The cafe is put to him in fictitious names, and concludes with the demand, Whether *Zayd* has, or has not, a right againft *Omar?* Under this is written the *Mufti*'s anfwer, which is fimply, *He has*, or, *He has not.*—*He can*, or, *He cannot.* At the bottom of the paper the *Mufti* figns his name, always fubfcribing himfelf, " the poor fervant of God."

Now, generally, this " poor fervant of God" never reads the cafe; but leaves the whole confideration of it to his *Fetfa Emini*, or deputy, who, as generally, is well bribed before-hand; he

puts

puts the cafe in his own manner, and inftructs the *Mufti* how he fhould fub-fcribe it. This is fo true, that there frequently appear oppofite *Fetfas* in the fame caufe ; fo that when a party thinks himfelf fecure on the *Mufti*'s decifion, he finds it of no effect in court, not liftened to, and often totally rejected.

One principal ufe to be made of them is, that when the judge is well fecured by a bribe, though on the unjuft fide : he will then lay a ftrefs on the decifion of the *Mufti* as perfectly juft, and fhelter his own injuftice under that fanction ; or at the worft, when contradictory *Fetfas* appear, he may favour the unjuft by exhorting the contending parties to an accommodation.

False witneffes fhould be punifhed according to the *Koran* ; however, that hap-

happens but feldom. Now and then a
notorious vagrant and offender, detected in his perjury, if it be in a caufe
againft fome great man, is led through
the ftreets on an afs, with his face towards the tail, and an infcription de-
claring him a *Scheat*, or falfe witnefs.
But even this is feldom feen, except it
be on the acceffion of a Sultan. A
new reign is generally ufhered in by
fome fuch examples. He declares he
will rule according to law, juftice, and
truth : as a proper warning therefore
to the people, the Vizir lays hold of
half a dozen of thefe witneffes, and
executes that pompous fentence. A punifhment fo trivial has rather a ridiculous than a ferious effect; fo that the
city of Conftantinople fwarms with
thefe wretches : but was it even as ferious as death, it may be juftly thought
their numbers would not diminifh; for

they

they are encouraged by the men of the law, as the principal means by which their judges, who are temporary, and almoſt annually removed, haſten to be rich, and able to ſubſiſt whilſt they are out of office.

To do their courts of law all the juſtice I can, I ſhall conclude with two remarkable deciſions, the one of which fell under my own knowledge; the other is, that I mentioned as having heard it well atteſted.

A Ship freighted at Alexandria by Turks, to bring them and their merchandize, conſiſting in rice and dates, to Conſtantinople, met with a violent ſtorm in the paſſage. The maſter told thoſe freighters who were on board, that he could not ſave the ſhip, nor their lives, but by throwing into the ſea all the goods on the deck.

THEY

THEY confented not only for them-felves, but for other freighters, who were at Conftantinople. When the fhip arrived there, thofe who had been on board joined with thofe who had not, to profecute the mafter of the fhip, in order to recover the value of the goods he had hove overboard. The *Moulah* of Galata, before whom he was fummoned, had the cafe fully reprefented to him, and his deputy, as ufual, had the promife of a reward.

WHEN the parties appeared, and the witneffes were examined, the *Moulah* reflected a-while, took down his book, and gravely opening it, told them, " the book declared, that the mafter fhould pay the true value of thofe very goods ;" that is, what the freighters could prove by witneffes any one would give for them, or what

they were really worth on board of the
ship, at the very moment the master
was conftrained to throw them into the
fea; the only means by which he could
fave the lives of his paffengers, amongft
whom were the perfons who now fued
him for it.

THE freighters ran out of court to
find witneffes; but the judge, who
knew it was no object on which any
would, or could dare to appear, without further hefitation gave his written
decree in favour of the mafter.

The fecond cafe was before a young
Cadi at Smyrna. A poor man claimed
a houfe which a rich man had ufurped.
The former held his deeds and documents
to prove his right, but the latter had
provided a number of witneffes to in-
validate them; and to fupport their
evi-

evidence the more effectually, he prefented the *Cadi* with a bag containing
five hundred ducats : the *Cadi* received
it. When it came to a hearing, the poor
man told his ftory, produced his writings, but wanted that moft effential
and only valid proof, witneffes.

The other, provided with witneffes,
laid his whole ftrefs on them, and on
his adverfary's defect in law, who could
produce none : he urged the *Cadi*
therefore to give fentence in his favour.

AFTER the moft preffing follicitations, the judge calmly drew out from
under his fopha the bag of five hundred ducats, which the rich man had
given him as a bribe ; faying to him
very gravely, "You have been much
" miftaken in the fuit ; for if the poor
" man could bring no witneffes in con-

" firmation

" firmation of his right, I myself can
" produce at least five hundred:" he
then threw him the bag with reproach
and indignation, and decreed the house
to the poor plaintiff.

Such instances may happen once in
an age, and deserve to be transmitted
to posterity; and, indeed, it is frequently related by the Turks themselves, as a most extraordinary and uncommon example.

CHAP.

CHAP. XI.

Of Ambaſſadors.—Their Audiences.

THE Turks have properly no idea of the law of nations: they conſider themſelves as the only nation on earth, and regulate their whole conduct with others on poſitive compact, ſpontaneous conceſſions, or uſage and cuſtom.

FOREIGN ambaſſadors, therefore, have no other ſecurity but written conceſſions of which they have copies, or ſuch privileges unwritten, as their predeceſſors made uſe of.

No longer than about fifty years ago, a Vizir, *Jin Aly Paſha*, thought them only civil ſpies, and was for removing the reſidence of ſuch trouble-

ſome

some guests to the Prince's-Island, nine miles from Constantinople.

As the trading powers remote from the Turks have no reciprocal advantages to grant them, their ambassadors in Turkey must submit to such terms as the government pleases to grant; and it is more surprising their capitulations or concessions have been so well observed, than if they had been totally neglected.

When there were only four ambassadors and one resident in Turkey, the character was supported with more dignity, and held in higher esteem by the Turks.

It is true, that their method of living was not the most sociable, but yet seemed the best calculated to engage

respect

respect and esteem. They copied the
manners of the great men among the
Turks; visiting rarely, but when they
did, it was with all the pomp of Eastern
ostentation : they dressed for that day in
the most sumptuous manner, had their
servants in their rich liveries, and five
or seven led horses, were it only to
cross a narrow street. They never appeared in the streets on common occasions, nor went over from Pera,
where their residence is, to Constantinople, but with all the ambassadorial
pomp and shew of representing the
person of a great monarch : if to visit
Sancta Sophia, or if to see a *Biram*, it
was with written commands furnished
to them by the Porte, who took care
to have them escorted and attended by
proper officers : in short, an ambassador was thought by the Lower Turks
to be a different being from the others

of

of his nation ; he was feldom feen ; and when he fhewed himfelf, he appeared to their eyes with the fplendor of the greateft officers in their own court.

WITHIN thefe thirty years, foreign minifters of the fecond order are increafed, and with the four ambaffadors make up ten.

THE urgent defire the princes of Chriftendom have fhewn to obtain the Grand Seignor's friendfhip at any rate, has greatly heightened the enormous vanity of the Porte ; and the increafed number of minifters has rendered the whole body lefs refpectable in the eyes of the people.

IF, perhaps, the fame maxims could have fubfifted, which had formerly been the rule of conduct between the four ambaffadors, the fame confequences

quences would have yet refulted; but, however neceffary it may be, men ufed to freedom, and to living in their own way, cannot eafily fubmit to fuch conftraint; and, indeed, there are few men who can fuffice to themfelves, or find a fufficient fund of entertainment in their own minds. A tacit compact may exift for a few years between four, but it is almoft impoffible among ten : fo that, as difficult as it was formerly to fee an ambaffador, you now meet them, or thofe of the fecond rank, who the people have not learnt to diftinguifh from them, at every corner of the ftreets, and in every part of the city. They make no fcruple, at prefent, to vifit Armenian, Greek, or Jew, to run over to a *Biram*, or any publick fhew : fometimes they meet with an infult, which they conceal; often with a pufh, which an in-

folent

folent Turk will crofs the way to treat them with; and are commonly followed with the epithet *Giaur*, infidel, the Turkifh epithet of deteftation and contempt.

If an accident of the graveft nature were to happen to them in Conftantinople, they can expect little or no fatisfaction; for the Porte would immediately throw it on their own imprudence, and tell them plainly, as they have done on fuch occafions, that ambaffadors fhould not expofe themfelves in a crowd, but have acquainted the Porte when they have bufinefs abroad, and then they would be properly fecured from infult.

In this fituation, where publick minifters are admitted on ftipulated conditions and only cuftomary privileges, as eafily withdrawn as granted, it behoves

hoves them more particularly to live with great circumspection; to support dignity with the Turks, and maintain decency and order in their families.

WHEREVER this conduct is duly observed and practised, few inconveniencies have ever arisen in Turkey. With such a demeanor the ambassador will find a satisfaction in himself, ease and order in his family, no revels amongst his domestics, no riots and no insults; and consequently no complaints are made to himself, or to the Porte, both of which will otherwise too frequently happen. The Turks have a homely proverb, which they have not improperly applied on such occasions : they say, "the "fish stinks first at the head;" meaning, That if the servant is disorderly, it is because the master is so.

THE dignity and importance affumed by ambaffadors in their reprefentative character was, for fome ages, it fhould feem, thought too much on a level with perfonal fovereignty, to admit of a fixed refidence, or permanency at any court.

IN thofe times, therefore, ambaffadors were fent only on very extraordinary, and temporary occafions; as, on fettling fome immediate important point in conteft; on a negotiation of marriages; or, more generally, on the conclufion of a long and bloody war; probably, as a publick mark of a fincere reconciliation, and as proper notice to the fubjects for their future conduct, authenticating the fecurity of their mutual intercourfe.

THE Turks religioufly obferve this latter very ancient cuftom: ambaffadors

dors never appear reciprocally but after a war; and wherever the frontier
is removed by the events of that war,
there the exchange of ambaſſadors from
the two courts is made.

As ſoon as the ambaſſador paſſes
on the Turkiſh frontier, the Grand
Seignor is conſidered as his hoſt, and
the officer who receives him, ſtiles him
the Grand Seignor's *Muſaphir*, his gueſt;
whether it is by ancient cuſtom amongſt
them, a remain of the general hoſpitality
of former times, or from the reſpect
in which they hold the office of ambaſſador; or whether it be only a pa-
rade of the Grand Seignor's power
and magnificence: whatever be the
motive, he is, however, immediately
provided with every neceſſary for his
journey, or a conſiderable allowance
given him in money, which is continued

nued during his ftay at Conftantinople.

THE ambaffador from a commercial power claims the fame right, and
enjoys it, though in a lefs degree; his
neceffaries, however, are fully fupplied : but as foon as the journey ends,
that emolument ceafes.

A VIZIR *Agà* is fent by the Porte
to receive him on the frontier, and to
conduct him fafe; his route is traced,
his refting-days in the feveral towns
are fixed, as alfo the *Thaym*, or allowance, he is to have for his fubfiftence,
and the number of horfes and carts allotted for his fervants and baggage : he
is treated with refpect and diftinction,
and as well provided as the road will
afford : the feveral diftricts of the
country furnifh the expence, and it
is

is passed at the treasury in the article of their contributions.

THE countries through which the Christian ministers pass, are generally gainers by it: for if one dollar is necessary to defray their expence, in adding another as a regale to the *Vizir-Aga*, they obtain from him a receipt for four, which they pass to the Grand Seignor as really paid.

IT is worth remarking with what incredible precaution, politeness, and lenity, the commissary, or *Vizir-Aga*, treats the Turks in the course of this journey; but when he comes among the Bulgarian Christians, if the ambassador does not interfere, he will not restrain himself from using them with the cruellest oppression and indignity.

THE

THE flattering profpect with which an ambaffador is iffued into the Grand Seignor's territories, gives him not only the hopes of a continuance, but of an agreeable reception and refidence near the throne of the prince.

WHEN he arrives, he is welcomed by a meffage from the Vizir, flattered and careffed by a number of Greeks, Armenians, and Jewifh dependants, with a fervility the loweft and bafeft, and moft difgufting.

THE firft opening of his function is to the Vizir : they both feat themfelves, the ambaffador on a ftool, the Vizir on the corner of his fofa ; mutual civilities pafs between them, without any variation in language fince the empire began. He is told, " that as long as his mafter obferves the laws of friendfhip with

with them, the Grand Seignor will cor-
refpond." The honours of the *Caftan,*
fweetmeats, coffee, fherbet, and per-
fume, are prefented to him ; but when
he departs they clap their hands, hifs him
out of the room, and two officers who
attend him, one on each fide, attempt
at half-way, to make him turn and falute the Vizir, who never ftirs off of
his corner : he who forgets his character may be furprifed into it ; but he
who does not, keeps on his pace, and
drives on his leaders.

On an occafion that offered of ad-
jufting the ceremonial with an ambaffador who thought himfelf offended,
this ufage was redreffed, and it is to
be hoped continues no longer.

How greatly foever fuch indecency
may fhock the delicacy of a man

jealous of his master's dignity, he has a much more humiliating scene to go through, at his audience of the Grand Seignor.

THE time appointed for the ambaſſador to be over the water * is the morning, at the break of day : on his landing he is received by the *Chiaux Paſhi*, or marſhal of the court, in a houſe deſtined for that purpoſe, the ſtairs of which are no better than a ladder, and the room fit rather for the reception of a Poliſh Jew than for a man of his dignity.

OFTEN, and indeed generally, the *Chiaux Paſhi* is not there at the ambaſſador's arrival; but the common ex-

---

* His houſe is in the ſuburb of Pera, ſeparated from Conſtantinople by a ſmall bay or creek of the Boſphorus; it is the port for ſhipping : this he muſt paſs whenever he comes into the city.

cuſe

-cufe is, that he is detain'd in the mofchee at his prayers.

WHEN the firft civilities are paffed over, an infinuation is made to the ambaffador, that he muft expect the *Chiaux Paſbi* will ride at his right hand. This part of the ceremonial, long con-tefted, but never given up by the Turks, except only when they have been beaten into it, leaves the ambaffador the fole refource of protefting; all other oppofition is in vain : he, however, in-fifts, that a gentleman of his retinue fhall ride at his left. With whatever feeming reluctance they admit this claim, if urged with proper refolution it fucceeds. It has indeed been often pro-ductive of ferious conteftation and dif-order in the march; and fometimes al-moft of a fufpenfion of the audience.

AFTER

AFTER waiting fome time in that miferable chamber at the water-fide, the Vizir's command arrives to let them know, that he is ready to depart from the Porte to the Seraglio. The cavalcade then begins, and marches in ftate to the Vizir's door, where, whether it rains, hails, or fnows, the ambaffador muft remain on horfeback in the ftreet to fee his pomp, and to falute his highnefs and his whole court, as they pafs by. When they are near the gate of the Seraglio, the ambaffador's train advances flowly : on his arrival, he finds the Vizir feated in the divan-chamber.

IN the middle of this chamber an old fquare ftool is prepared for the ambaffador ; and he is there fixed, if the ftool can fupport him, at leaft for two hours, hearing the decifion of caufes he does not underftand ; tho' if it be a

pay-

pay-day for the Janifaries and Spahis, and this the Turks generally chufe, he is entertained with feeing about two thoufand four hundred yellow bags of money told out and diftributed; and this lafts at leaft twice two hours; fo that in a cold day, without a fur, his very vitals may freeze; and at any time the fpine of his back muft fuffer cruelly, for he has nothing to lean againft to fupport or eafe it.

AFTER this part of the fcene is over a new one fucceeds : the dinner is ferved; the ambaffador fits on his ftool, the Vizir on his elevated fopha; a round table is brought between them, at each fide of which is placed a handkerchief folded up to wipe the mouth and hands; fifty difhes, fucceeding each other, every half minute, come in like a torrent; a head-fervant ftands

near

near the ambaſſador with his arms
bare : his office is to tear a fowl in
pieces, and to lay the choiceſt mor-
ſels of it before them, all which
he performs with his fingers; he com-
mends without ceaſing the excellent
dinner, whilſt the Vizir preſſes his
gueſt to eat, and, perhaps, enters into
familiar converſation with him : and
at the laſt, to crown the repaſt, one
draught of ſherbet is ſerved.

THE Grand Seignor all the while
peeps through a dark window to ſee
the whole entertainment, and as ſoon as
it is over retires to his audience-room.

THE *Chiaux Paſhi* enters with his
Talkiſh, or order in writing, to the
Vizir, to tell him, that the monarch
is on his throne : he receives it with
the utmoſt ſubmiſſion, firſt touches his

fore-

forehead with it, then kiffes it, and having read it, puts it into his breaft, and
departs.

AFTER his departure, the ambaffador is told he muft crofs the court-
yard to go to the audience : he is pre-
ceded by the *Chiaux Pafhi* with all his
officers and attendants richly clad.

BUT he does not immediately enter
the audience-room ; he is ftopt in the
court-yard, where, under a tree, by
way of bench, is a fingle old board,
on which, at other times, grooms,
hoftlers, and fcullions lie to fun themfelves, though it fometimes ferves them
for lefs decent purpofes : on this, that
he fhould not wait too long ftanding,
they defire him to fit until he is vefted
with the *Caftan.* They do not examine whether this bench is wet or

D 4   dry,

dry, clean or dirty, nor whether it rains or fnows. As foon as the ceremony of vefting is over, two *Capigis Pafhis* feize him by the fhoulders, and conduct him in. He finds the monarch at one corner placed on his fopha, higher by much than common, and covered with a canopy; his legs rather pending: at his fide lies a rich fword, and fome regalia. He eyes the ambaffador afkew, hears his harangue, which, were it fpoken with the eloquence of Cicero, would gain little attention: nor does it import in what language it is pronounced; for the real one is given in to the Vizir before, tranflated by the Drugoman, or interpreter of the Porte; who, after the ambaffador has done, repeats it extempore, in the Turkifh language, to the Grand Seignor.

THE

THE monarch fpeaks a few words to the Vizir, who advances towards the middle of the room, and anfwers the ambaffador in their ufual common-place language: this the interpreter explains, and thus the audience finifhes, and the ambaffador is difmiffed.

AFTER all is over, he expects to be delivered from the tedioufnefs of that day, and without further obftacle to mount his horfe, and be gone: he mounts, it is true; but in the fecond quadrangle of the Seraglio, he is ftopped, and obliged to wait on horfeback under a tree, until the Vizir paffes before him on his return home; and then he is fuffered to depart.

PERSONAL vanity, or national pride, has not permitted Chriftian writers to fet this ceremonial in its true light; nay,

nay, some ambaſſadors have been for ſoftening and palliating the worſt of its indecorum. They have gone ſo far as even to pretend, that the preſents they carry, and which they are obliged to give at every audience, reflect honour on themſelves as the givers, but not on the Turks as receivers.

WHOEVER is acquainted with the Oriental practice, and knows the oſtentation, pride, and haughtineſs of Turkiſh government, muſt know that they look upon, and conſider ſuch preſents as actual tributes.

THERE is one of their neighbouring courts who have taken it in a true, and a becoming ſenſe ; and ſtipulated in their treaties, that preſents ſhall be reciprocal, that they ſhall be exchanged, but not inſolently exacted.

WE

WE may be furprized that other courts have not followed this exam-ple; but what appears more furprizing, is, that very court never took into ferious confideration the nature of the ceremonial, and the indecent ufage of their reprefentatives. It is furely ftrange that the Imperial court fhould have neglected it at the treaty of Paf-farowitz, fince they then thought it expedient to make it an exprefs article, " that their ambaffadors fhould appear " at thefe audiences in what drefs they " pleafed." For before that time they were obliged to ufe the Turkifh habit. They moft certainly were not informed of all the mortifying particulars I have related, or they chofe to pafs over with contempt, what might appear to them only the vain oftenta-tion of a Turkifh court.

I MUST

I MUST, however, obferve, that except the mortifications which attend
an audience, it may on the whole be
faid, that if ambaffadors are not in-
cumbered with difagreeable bufinefs,
fuch as may interfere with the interefts
of Turkifh individuals, or of the Porte
in general, they may live in Turkey
with great dignity, eafe, and fatif-
faction.

C H A P.

CHAP. XII.

Miscellaneous observations on the manners of the Turks.

IT may be a queſtion, whether men, before they aſſembled together into cities, or formed ſocieties within the encloſure of towns, were not more pure and undefiled in their manners, and endowed with greater rectitude of morals. We have reaſon to think they were, from the hiſtory of mankind; and our own obſervations will generally confirm us in the opinion.

THE more men are together, the more their wants increaſe, the more their paſſions are exalted; and they ſeek every means to ſupply the one, and ſatisfy the other.

HENCE,

HENCE, I once concluded, arofe the difference between the city and the ruftick Turk : the former, artful and defigning ; the latter, open and fimple, though equally with the other affecting an air of contempt and backwardnefs in their fervices towards Chriftians ; the refult, I fuppofe, of education and religion.

FROM this appearance I was tempted to enquire as diligently as I could, whether the Turks, living in feparate hamlets, unconnected and unmixed with Greeks, Armenians, and Jews, were more virtuous and honeft than in cities and villages, where all thefe religions were profeffed, and the different fects herding indifcriminately together, made, as it were, but one people. I put the queftion to feveral, without obtaining a fatisfactory anfwer : at length

the

the fame *Effendi*, with whom I converfed concerning the *Koran*, who was
a native of Bofnia, had lived long in
his own country, and who feemed always to think freely in matters of religion, anfwered me, that they fcarce
knew in a mere Turkifh village, what
trick, deceit, or roguery, were amongft
each other; that having obferved and
compared the difference between them,
and the villages in which Turks and
Greeks were mixed, he found by undoubted obfervation, that the latter
tainted the whole community; that
they taught the Turks to deceive, to
embroil their own families, feduced
them into proceffes and law-fuits, infpired the *Cadi* of the diftrict with the
luft of gain, and, that they might have
his protection, became his inftruments in the iniquitous means of ac-
quiring it.

HE

HE added, that nothing could furnish better examples, or more illustrate the subject, than the manners of the Turcomen, bands of whom are itinerant through Asia, like the ancient patriarchs, and amongst whom fraud and deceit are almost unknown; but yet if they happen to mix with the Armenians or Jews in villages or towns, they become as consummately artful as any of them; but then they seldom dare return to their own community.

BUT how plausible soever this may seem, I should think, on farther reflexion and better acquaintance with Turkish manners, juster causes may be assigned for their depravity; because where men are exposed by a corrupt administration of justice, or otherwise, to oppression, self-defence and necessity will teach them cunning and deceit, without other instructors.

HE

He muſt be the righteous *Cadi* of Smyrna, who will not ſollicit bribes, nor foment litigation, and excite law-ſuits, ſince by theſe means he acquires wealth almoſt without a riſque; and he muſt be a moſt righteous *Paſha*, indeed, who, in traverſing a country, will not plunder for himſelf in every town and village thro' which he paſſes, under the pretence of taking his due; or who will hinder his retinue and depen-dants from plundering in like manner. As therefore the people cannot prevent the one or the other by force, they will naturally exert their whole facul-ties to eſcape oppreſſion; but lies, hy-pocriſy, and evaſion, are their only inſtru-ments of defence. Habituated to this, from one ſtep they eaſily take the other, and extend it thro' all their dealings: thus the tyranny and the example of their ſuperiors muſt be allowed to contri-

bute greatly to their degenerate manners.

THE changes of *Paſhas* from one
government to the other, ſometimes
from the confines of Perſia to the
confines of Europe, is one of the
great grievances, and, indeed, almoſt
the greateſt the ſubjects ſuffer under
what may properly be called miniſtry,
or government in Turkey; for although
a *Paſha* on this occaſion is limited to an
allowance, which the country furniſhes
from each diſtrict, in the ſame manner,
and with the ſame indemnification, as
they defray the journey of an ambaſſador; and that the orders of the Sultan
ſtrictly prohibit any farther exactions; yet
if he finds an effectual venal protection
at the Porte, or that the interior of the
Seraglio has the power, and are ſufficiently corrupt to ſhare in his extortions,

he

he gives little attention to the sovereign's orders, or to his stipulated *Thaym* or allowance; but regardless whether they are Turks, Christians, or Jews, who are the prey of his rapacity, he drains the very vitals of the country, from the beginning of his journey to the end, and plunders without remission or remorse.

For six years, during the power of Bechir the Black *Kiſlar-Aga* who was executed in sultan Machmut's reign, this evil became enormous; every *Paſha* strove to be his creature, and continually gave him, or his dependants, large sums for their support and protection. Commit what outrage he pleased, it was in vain for the inhabitants of those districts through which he passed to cry out against him, to come in bands with *Arz Mahzars*, or

E 2   gene-

general reprefentations of their grievances to the Grand Seignor.

If they delivered their complaints
to the Porte, the Vizir dared not lay
them before the Sultan, dreading exile,
or worfe : if prefented to the Sultan in
his way to the mofchee, it was either
received from the complainants by the
Black *Kiflar-Aga*, or immediately put
into his hands and fuppreffed. The
proceeding of the miniftry on thefe
occafions was to tire out the complainants with delays, and then exhort them
to return home, and truft to the Vizir
for fatisfaction and redrefs.

After the execution of this Black,
the Grand Seignor fent out the thunder of his commands, with threats of
difgrace and punifhment againft all
Pafhas guilty of rapine, prohibiting it

6   for

for the future, enjoining them at the same time to give no presents to his ministers; for that, he found, was the pretence under which their rapine was exercised.

THE evil ceased for a time : it never continues in one state, but ebbs and flows, and shifts according to the variation of power in men about the Sultan, who may sometimes oblige it to intermit, like the paroxysms of a fever; but his politico-medical abilities are not sufficient to put an effectual stop to the return.

NOTWITHSTANDING the general abuse of power, the venality and the other defects which may be found in the Turkish government, their interior policy, or provision for the security of individuals, is excellent, and worthy of imitation.

E 3 HIGH-

Highway robberies, houfe-breaking, even pilfering, are almoft unknown amongft them; be it in time
of peace or of war, the roads are as
fecure as their houfes; the whole empire, efpecially through the high roads,
may be always traverfed with the utmoft fafety; and, confidering the continual run of paffengers, it is wonder-
ful the very few tragical accidents which
happen; not one, perhaps, in feveral
years.

This fecurity poffibly may be founded on the fame principle on which our
divifions of hundredths and tythings
were firft inftituted.

For, in like manner, the whole
Turkifh empire is divided into different diftricts of country, which are
anfwerable for every robbery or murder

der committed within its limits; they are therefore vigilant to prevent either, as they foon feel the weight of a fevere and fummary juftice : for on the leaft pretence, a great officer of the Porte is immediately difpatched to take their examination; the diftrict pays the expence of this inqueft, whether they exculpate themfelves or not; nor does he depart, until he takes with him almoft their laft farthing.

THE meaner Turks, however, muft have fome motive fuperior to that of fear to reftrain them; for the country is fo vaft, and the roads are fo open, from one extremity of the empire to the other, that they might rob and murder with impunity, and fave themfelves in fome diftant province, notwithftanding every human precaution to prevent it.

E 4   I HAVE

I have known a Franc in his own drefs, who travelled alone round the camp of a Turkifh army affembling for the Perfian war, and paffed thro' it, without being afked a queftion, or receiving the leaft interruption in his journey.

Whether the Turks look on ftealing with difdain, as a bafenefs unworthy of human nature ; or whether they do indeed fear the laws, which, however, are not very fevere ; houfe-breaking, or pilfering, by Turks fcarce ever happens in Conftantinople.

In that city the Bulgarians are thofe moft to be apprehended ; they are generally the thieves ; but yet you may live there with fecurity, and your doors remain almoft continually open.

The Greeks feldom rob any thing confiderable ; but their fingers are as nim-

nimble as their genius is fprightly : they will pilfer. Every little, they fay, accumulates until it becomes a heap; and that little is fcarce miffed, or, if miffed, is not an object worth enquiring after. In general, however, many of the Ifland-Greeks are fober and honeft, except with their tongues; for they will fay and unfay, invent and tergiverfate, with a marvellous promptnefs and fluency.

BIRTH does not recommend to great offices in Turkey; merit and abilities may exalt the cottager to the higheft office of the empire.

THE Turks do not think that blood can convey either the fame faculties of the mind, or the fame moral qualities from the anceftor to the fucceffor; but they believe that virtue, wifdom, cou-

courage, riches, in fhort, every diftri-
bution of gifts and talents, and all the
different ranks and orders of men, are
decreed and allotted by the Supreme
Being to the different individuals of
fociety, without any regard to particular families; fo that even the defcendants of their prophet, who are
very numerous, remain generally in
the loweft and moft abject ftate, en-
joying only fome trifling privileges,
which can never influence their fortune.

I OBSERVED, however, that fome families are refpected by the people,
merely for the merit of their anceftors. One, indeed, the defcendant of
Ibrahim Kan, is particularly diftinguifhed by all ranks; and fome pretend,
that he is vifited twice a year by the
Sultan himfelf.

IBRA-

IBRAHIM was Vizir to Mahomet II.
That Sultan, when he had fubdued
Walachia, left Adrianople, and paffed
over into Afia to chaftife feveral princes
who had revolted from him. He was
ftopped in his return from that expe-
dition by an impoftor, who pretended
to be Muftapha, the fon of Bajazet,
loft or killed in the battle againft Ta-
merlane. This impoftor was befieging
the city of Nicea in Bythinia, where
Mahomet attacked and routed him;
but, foon after, was taken ill of a dy-
fentery, and died. His fon Amurath
was then in Europe warring againft the
Bulgarians. In this critical fituation,
the Vizir Ibrahim conveyed advice to
Amurath of his father's death, but
concealed it forty-one days from the
knowledge of the army: public bufinefs went on as if he was alive till
Amurath arrived.

FOR

FOR this important service, Ibrahim had the title of *Kan*, almost equivalent to that of king, conferred on him, with many honours and large emoluments ; all of which were confirmed to him and his descendants by Solyman Canauni, or the Lawgiver, commonly called the Magnificent. This family bears the name of Ibrahim Kan Oglu : they have built and endowed an incredible number of religious houses, and public *Khans* for the reception of travellers, of which they are perpetual inspectors and directors. They are, in like manner as the Sultan himself, exempt from mixing blood by marriage with any other family, and only have concubines. They can refuse to accept any office in the administration; and I have been told, that they have the only hereditary title in the empire, that of Great Huntsman, or Great Falconer.

Amongst the defcendants of Vizirs, the Kiuporli family, of whom there are few remaining ; and in the law, that of Damas-Zade, whofe anceftor was the firft *Mufti* after the taking of Conftantinople ; are both infinitely ref-pected by the people.

. In general, I think to have feen, that the people pay regard to the defcend-ants of *Pafhas*, or of confiderable *Effendis :* perhaps the attention fhewn them, may be in proportion to their wealth and connections, or their pub-lick donations.

But what is certain, and feems an effential mark of diftinction, is, that any man in the empire who marries a lady defcended from a *Pafha*, or an eminent perfon in the law, or, indeed, of any other profeffion, muft content him-

himfelf without any other wife; nor does he dare have a concubine in the fame houfe. I have feen it carried farther by a Vizir who was thus married; for though he had his concubines ouf of the houfe, he was obliged to conceal it very carefully from his lady.

THE Turks are ftrong in their parental affections, and the children reciprocal in their obedience, fubmiffion, and filial duty: fuch education leads them to much feeming modefty with their fuperiors, and the young men to great veneration towards the old. Perhaps this, with their total, and very early feparation from women, has infufed that remarkable bafhfulnefs in their behaviour towards them, and occafions that refpect with which they treat the fex.

A MAN, meeting a woman in the ftreets, turns his head from her, as if it were

were forbidden to look on her : they seem to detest an impudent woman, shun and avoid her.

·Any one, therefore, among the Christians, who may have discussions or altercations with Turks, if he has a woman of spirit, a virago for his wife, sets her to rout and brow-beat them; and by this means not unfrequently gains his point.

The highest disgrace and shame would attend a Turk who should rashly lift his hand against a woman; all he can venture to do, is to treat her with harsh and contemptuous words, or to go off.

The sex lay such stress on this privilege, that they are frequently apt to indulge their passion to excess, to be most unreasonable in their claims, and

2   vio-

violent and irregular in the purfuit of them. They will importune, teaze, and: infult a judge on the bench; or even: the Vizir at his divan: the officers of juftice do not know how to refent their turbulence: and it is a general obfervation, that to get well rid of them, they often give them their caufe.

A REMARKABLE fcene was acted by the women at the acceffion of fultan Muftapha.

His Vizir, Regib Mehemet Pafha, who, towards the end of the preceding reign, had found himfelf unftable in his poft, and who expected daily by the internal intrigues of the Seraglio to be depofed, neglected to provide the neceffary fupply of corn and rice for the yearly confumption of the city, tho' an effential part of his duty; the

pub-

publick granaries were almoft empty,
and lefs rice than ufual had been imported : however, contrary to his expectation, he found himfelf invefted with full
power by the new Sultan, and rendered
abfolute ; but then it was too late in the
feafon for him to introduce plenty. Bread
mixed up with oats, barley, millet
and fand, was dear and fcarce ; and rice
hardly to be bought at any price.

In this diftrefs, the men bore their
want with paffive and fullen difcontent ;
but the women, impatient and daring,
affembled in a confiderable body, and
with hammers, chiffels, and files, attacked the magazines, where they
pretended rice was in great quantities
monopolized. No oppofition could ftop
them ; and whilft the publick officers
were perplexed what party to take,
they broke open locks, bars, and

bolts, entered the magazines, took with them such quantities as they could carry off, and went away unmolested.

None of these female rioters were ever punished, as far as we knew; and if you spoke to a grave Turk about them, he would tell you with a sneer, it was only a mutiny of turbulent women.

I have heard it averred by a person of great veracity, who had lived for some years in a Sultan's *Harem* of the blood-royal, that it was impossible for women to behave with more decency and modesty than the Turkish ladies did, and that they treated each other with the greatest politeness.

In families of the higher class, where education is more exalted, where read-
ing

ing of their own language, or the Arabian, is probably cultivated; precepts of virtue and morality, of gentle demeanor and good breeding, chaftity of manners, with whatever decorates the fex, and renders them amiable, may be inculcated.

But, in general, it is known that the women who are fold or prefented to their great men, either for wives or concubines, have their price and value regulated not only according to the beauty or form of the perfon, but according to thofe acquired graces, and artificial allurements, which they have induftriously been taught: thefe are always fuch as may conduce to raife and inflame the paffions. Hence they teach them vocal and inftrumental mufic; certain peculiar affectations in their gait; and often fuch dances as

F 2

to a modeſt ſpectator would appear
rather indecent.

FACTS, by which we can be thoroughly aſſured of the female charac-
teriſtic in Turkey, are difficult to come
at ; accident may throw them in our
way: one fell in mine, which, if it did
not ſeem to ſuggeſt too uncharitable
and ungenerous a way of thinking,
might lead us to judge of the whole:
Crimine ab uno diſce omnes.

THE *Harems* of great men, that is,
all the ladies, and their attendants,
are in the ſummer ſeaſon frequently
permitted to walk abroad an airing on
foot, either in the fields on the borders
of the Boſphorus, or other ſuch public places : theſe parties generally con-
ſiſt of twenty or thirty, and ſometimes
of forty or fifty women, according to
the

the opulence of the master; and they are always attended by the guardians of their chastity the Black Eunuchs.

It is common with the Francs or Christian foreigners to pass over to the Asiatic side of the Bosphorus for an evening's recreation. Two of them went thither as usual with ladies, attended by Janizaries and servants. As they were returning slowly, they heard a confused noise of female voices following them. Their curiosity prompted them to see, as well as hear: they turned short, and stopped. They found these voices proceeded from two *Harems*, composed of near forty women: their faithful watchmen the Blacks attended on each side, guarding them, though at some distance. One of the spectators stood longer, and with more earnestness to contemplate their figure and

F 3   beha-

behaviour. He thought they would rather avoid than approach him. He was miftaken : for on a fudden, he found himfelf feized by a feeming dapper brifk girl, followed by the whole band; who firft accofting him with indelicate amorous expletives, and after with foothing and tender expreffions, attempted to unravel the myftery of his whole drefs.

The force of the conflict, and the army of females about him, left him but the fingle refource of laughter and ftruggles : he could not debarrafs himfelf from fuch numerous, determined affailants by threats nor intreaties; nor vanquifh the vehemence of their curiofity, by reprefenting the fhame to which they expofed themfelves, by a behaviour fo grofly and fo publickly indecent.

An

An old Janizary attending him, ftood at fome diftance, as it were in amaze. His Mahometan bafhfulnefs would not permit him to advance towards women; nor would he have dared to lay his hands on them: all he ventured at in the fray, was to work up a ftern countenance towards the Black Eunuchs, and with a Stentorian voice to exclaim againft them and their wards, telling them they were the guardians of proftitutes, rather than of modeft women; and urging them to exert themfelves to free the man from fuch importunate violators.——All in vain.

A young man of the company, a foreigner, either envying the other, or prompted by compaffion at feeing his untoward fituation, boldly advanced; and as he fpoke more Turkifh than the perfon engaged, began to ex-

poftulate

postulate with them, sometimes with a smile, and sometimes with a frown. Whether his countenance, his form, or his greater youth, were more attractive, they at once quitted hold of their first prey, flew on him with eager and inquisitive hands, and whilst he underwent the same treatment, gave the other time to reach his boat. The youth, robust and active, disengaged himself after much struggling, and at length with difficulty saved himself by flight; happy not to have been quite stripped, and to have been able to join the company with decent covering.

I must add, as the general opinion, and what I have always heard, that the Turkish ladies in general are rather immodest and libidinous. This may possibly be applied with some justice to those women who are sold, or

pre-

prefented to the great and the opulent,

HENCE a reflection occurred to me,
which I have often made to fenfi-
ble Roman Catholicks in their own
country, that a convent education for
young ladies deftined to act a focial
part, and live amongft mankind, is
improper and dangerous,

THEY are kept up reclufe, debar-
red the converfe of men, until they
are almoft nubile : if they drop a word
concerning them, it is reckoned indecent, and draws on them the frown of
their fuperior; even to think there is
a fex different from their own, is almoft
criminal; in fhort, every natural fenti-
ment muft be fuppreffed.

THEIR teachers do not reflect, that
human nature craves after what is forbidden;

bidden; that unextinguishable curiosity works up the imagination, and inflames the passions; and that, therefore, young women just freed from confinement, and entering the world without experience and without knowledge, must fall a prey to the first bold invader of their affections. Such an education frequently occasions either a shipwreck of their virtue, or a disproportioned and unhappy marriage : thus a youth of constraint ends in a life of misery. Let them converse early with men, and mix betimes with that general society in which they are to pass their lives; for lessons of modesty must make the stronger impression on them, when they see the mischiefs and misfortunes which attend the want of it; it is adding example to precept.

WHENCE

WHENCE the idea of the tranfcendant beauty of Turkifh women has arifen, is difficult to fay, unlefs it be from the warm imaginations of inventive travellers, who have raifed thefe beauteous phantoms, fketched their forms, and became enamoured with originals they never faw.

HENCE, throughout Chriftendom, the fair Circaffian has been the fubject of romance and fong; when, perhaps, there are not two men in it who ever faw one of thefe Venus's. It is certainly impoffible in Turkey: for from infancy to old age, fcarce a fingle trace of a Turkifh woman's face is perceptible. No adult maiden is ever vifible, nor no married woman, except to their parents, brethren, or hufband. As foon as they put on the *Macremma*, or Veil of Modefty, every

fea-

feature of their face is covered, except a small part of the nose and eyes; and some have carried that custom to such an extreme of delicacy, that when they feed their poultry, if there is cocks amongst their hens, they will not appear before them without it. If Praxiteles or Apelles, with an angelic conception added to their art, had met the two *Harems* on the borders of the Bosphorus, they could not have formed the least idea of the contour, form, or proportion of the face and features of one person in them; all to be distinguished was black or blue eyes, and a faint perception of the complexion of the skin.

However, as they carefully preserve their faces from the harsh influence of the different changes of the air; as their hours are regular, and they are

not

not expofed to a nocturnal atmofphere, or to 'the mixed warm exhalations of crowded rooms; we might expect, that if the original formation is beautiful, and nature has given them a fair and vivid complexion, thofe charms would be preferved many years, and only fuffer a gradual decay at the approach of old age.

THE Greek women are not tied down to the rigorous obfervance of a Turkifh reftraint; they vifit frequently, and, except in the ftreet, their faces are not muffled up in the *Macremma*. Of thefe we may fpeak with certainty; they have, for the moft part, good features and pleafing countenances; but in general rather a tarnifhed than a fair complexion.

THE one and the other, indeed, become decayed before nature intended it:

it : they deſtroy the whole texture of
the ſolids by the too frequent uſe of
hot baths, and they haſten too early to
matrimony.

The Turkiſh women are obliged to
bathe by the precepts of their religion ;
the Greeks by cuſtom, luxury, and
choice.

The numbers of publick baths at
Conſtantinople are prodigious, and of
the private ones incredible. The laſt,
indeed, are the higheſt indulgence of
luxury and vanity ; for all who are any
ways in eaſy circumſtances, have convenient baths of their own ; and among
the more opulent it is common to have
them moſt magnificent.

The Turks and Jews may, on account of their religion, be held excuſe-
able,

able, even in the extravagance of that expence; but the Greeks and Armenians have only empty vanity to apologize for it: they neverthelefs indulge that vanity, although they tremble that a Turk fhould know they dare imitate them, or outvie them in magnificence.

THE publick and private baths may differ in their ornaments and dimenfions, but do not vary in their models and ftructure; they feem formed merely for a decent and a modeft ufe.

THEY confift of three rooms: the firft is a large hall, where the bathers wait till the bath is ready for them; the fecond is a room in which they drefs and undrefs; and the third is the bathing-room. The bath itfelf is a large ftone or marble ciftern, of capacity fufficient to receive a man lying in

it

it at his full length : in the public baths
a number of thefe cifterns are placed :
they are fupplied with water by feveral pipes conducted through the walls.
The bath-man, or woman, according
to the fex of the bather, attends, wafhes,
rubs, and dries them with furprifing
dexterity and art, fuppling and ftretch-
ing the joints in fuch a manner, that
imagination would perfuade one they
diflocate every part of the body ; and
yet this operation occafions rather an
agreeable fenfation.

THE women are generally attended
by a female flave, or fervant of their
own : they undrefs in the room appointed for that purpofe, and put on
their bathing-cloaths, which are ufually of blue and white checked cotton.
After they have bathed, they return
again into this room ; there is a fopha

6   in

in it; on which they throw themselves
and are dreffed, and when fufficiently
cool, return into the hall. Thofe who
chufe it, have the bath heated on purpofe for them; but two never bathe together in the fame ciftern; and different hours of admittance are affigned
to the different perfons who intend
bathing the fame day. Indeed, the
heat will not admit of a long ftay in the
bathing ciftern, though moft who ufe
them indulge to too great an excefs.

It is cuftomary in Turkey to marry
young boys of thirteen or fourteen to
girls of eleven or twelve, and fometimes even under that age : the practice
is common among all fects of religion.
They are joined together on the good
faith of their parents or relations; for
they are never permitted to fee each
other before the nuptial night. Various

tricks, it is faid, have been played on thefe occafions among the Greeks and Armenians: the lame, the deformed, and the blind, were often matched to beauty and vigour. When the parties impofed on complained, the contrivers of their difappointment would anfwer with a compliment to their beauty and good qualities, and a profeffion, that their inducement to this fraud was only a defire to improve the race. This injury is the greater, as Chriftians cannot eafily obtain a divorce: but at prefent, indeed, the Greek girls become daily wifer, and generally infift on a peep at a window, or in a room; and they are not fo fcrupuloufly delicate, as not to unveil to their fuitor. Nay, they often marry without confulting farther than their own inclination.

THE

THE Turks are more conveniently circumftanced in regard of the matrimonial tie. The Grand Seignor is intirely exempt from it; he claims the privilege Mahomet referved for himfelf; and to avoid a formal contract of affinity, or, in the Turkifh phrafe, not to mix blood with any family in his empire, he has no wife, but only concubines. The firft of them who brings him a fon is called the *Sultana Hafeki:* fhe is crowned with flowers, takes on her the prerogatives of a wife, and governs in the *Harem.*

OTHER Turks are allowed four wives. They may marry, as it is called, *Kabbin*; that is, they appear before the tribunal of juftice, declare the woman to be their wife, and enter into an obligation, that whenever they fhall think proper to difmifs her, they

will

will maintain the children, and give
her a certain ſtipulated ſum, which
they proportion either to their circumſtances, or to the time they judge it
may be convenient for them to coha-
bit with her. It is no ſtain to a woman's character that ſhe is thus put
away, nor much impediment to her
finding another huſband.

Amongst the middling or common people, the ſum is generally very
moderate, and runs from * five thouſand to a hundred thouſand aſpers.

Hence you find few of this rank
who have more than one wife at one
time; for they frequently change, diſ-
miſſing one and taking another, as it
is done with little trouble, and at no
great expence.

* An hundred and twenty aſpers is two ſhil-
lings and ſixpence.

The

THE opulent have often three or four wives, and perhaps many concubines; but if they chuse to abide by the more laudable part of the law, and keep only to wives, it is equally convenient; for they may alternate and change as often as the number will admit.

AFTER divorce they may retake the same woman a second, but not the third time, unless she has been married to another husband. No man can marry a divorced woman sooner than four months and a half after a total separation from the former husband.

THE man may oblige the divorced woman to nurse any infant she has borne him till it is two years old.

FROM hence we may readily account why few common prostitutes are to be
found

found amongſt the Turks : their very religion furniſhes them, whatever their conſtitution and temper may be, with a ſuper-abundant variety and ſatiety of women.

WHETHER from ſuch a promiſcuous uſe of women, or from whatever other cauſe it may ariſe, there is not that number of children in Turkiſh families which the idea of polygamy naturally ſuggeſts : nay, it may be affirmed, that they have not, in general, as many children as are found in common families of Chriſtians or Jews. Giul Achmet, who died *Paſha* of the Morea, had the greateſt number I have heard of in one Turkiſh family ; he had nineteen. Among Chriſtians, I knew one family of twenty-one, and another of twenty-three children, by one mother in each family.

MAY

MAY it not from hence be inferred, that polygamy is deviating from the law of nature? Is it not a ftrong prefumptive argument to prove, that as the number of male and female births run almoft in equal proportion; fo to keep up a conftant order of population, one woman only fhould be allowed to one man.

NAY, that this fuppofed proportion between the number of men and women holds true, may be juftly concluded from the obvious confequence of polygamy in Turkey; for to what other caufe can it be attributed, that they have not a fufficient fupply of women for their men? It is evident, that throughout the vaft extent of the Mahometan dominions they have it not, but that women are daily imported amongft them from other countries: they

ar

are a merchandize of an exotic production; the price of which ebbs and flows, according to the plenty or scarcity of the market.

WAR supplies this want by the numbers of female captives it furnishes: the Turks in their excursions are very eager at seizing them; and women are then plenty and cheap.

BUT what is strange, in time of peace the mere poverty and misery of their neighbours the Georgians, who are a kind of Christians, oblige that wretched people to furnish spontaneously their choicest maidens to the Mahometan markets, as their country must starve and perish without that species of commerce.

I CANNOT help observing how the world has been imposed upon and

8   amused

amufed with romantic ftories of the
artful and fubtle amorous intrigues carried on with Turkifh ladies. It is
as eafy to fcalade the heaven, as to
come at them: their apartments are
fortreffes, moft of them furrounded with
high walls, and they have not a window
which opens towards the ftreet; their
guardians are ever about them; and the
fecret can never be with-held from ten,
twenty, or double that number of
other women. They feldom or ever
walk the ftreets but in infancy or old
age; the rich are never feen: and were
opportunities to offer, which might
render it poffible for a Chriftian to
attempt an intrigue with a Turkifh
woman, he knows, that on detection
immediate death is his doom; and
that thofe who have been acceffary,
whether by encouragement or conni-
vance, fhare the fame fate.

It

It is difficult to give a juft account of the manner in which Turks, men or women, fpend their time when at home. Some of the former are undoubtedly ftudious, though moft of them feem ever bufied about money affairs and their perfonal intereft. When they are difpofed to enjoy fome relaxation or amufement among themfelves, the diverfions are ftory-telling, quaint jokes, chefs or draughts, and not unfrequently dancers and muficians, who ply in the different parts of the town for employment.

If none of the company is fufficiently facetious to entertain the reft with that low ribaldry in which they chiefly delight, they find fome dependant, whether Greek, Armenian, or Jew, who acts the part. Thefe take their place, in the middle of the room, on

their

their knees, and tell their ſtory, or repeat their joke; whilſt the grave Turk ſmokes his pipe in the corner of the ſopha, and comes out now and then with a ſmile, or a dry laugh.

GAMING they highly deteſt, and look on a *Coſmerbas*, a gameſter who plays for money, worſe than a common thief; no being is more odious in their eyes: they, therefore, never touch a chefs-table, or a draught-board, but for mere amuſement.

THEIR dancers they have from amongſt the Greeks; and what appears moſt unaccountable, unleſs we ſuppoſe it ariſes from the abſolute contempt in which they hold that people, is, how it happens that the Turks, born in the ſame climate, and mixed ſome centuries with them, have not yet adopted their
mirth

mirth and jollity; and how they can hear and fee them continually dancing and finging, without ftirring a leg themfelves, or joining in a chorus. Such of them as ufe the fea, are of neceffity mixed amongft fome hundreds of Greek mariners, who when they are on fhore, or, indeed, on board their fhip, are never without mufick and dancing; yet a Turk is never found revelling with them.

Nay, the men of high, or even middling rank among them, feem to look on dancing, in refpect of themfelves, as unbecoming the dignity of man; befitting only the meaneft and moft abandoned of their fpecies: they think with the ancient Romans—*Nemo fere faltat fobrius nifi forte infanit:* " No one dances, unlefs he is drunk or mad."

THEY

THEY therefore never fall into that excefs, except when they are quite mad, or almoft dead drunk; indeed they never are fo by halves; and then they feldom fail to call in, at leaft, the publick dancers, whofe obfcene geftures prohibit a glance of a chafte eye.

THEIR own vocal and inftrumental mufick they have in efteem. The vocal has a fharp, fhrill tone, as it were, through the nofe of the finger; the voice is neverthelefs pleafing; and with all the difcordancy of inftruments, there is yet fomething great and martial in the combined founds of the whole.

HOWEVER, no Turk of any fafhion will deign to touch an * inftrument;

* A well known Greek Vaivode, or prince, of Moldavia, obtained that dignity by playing on the guitarre to one Ephraim, or Ibrahim Effendi, a favourite of the Grand Seignor's.

they

they hire minftrels, or have women, or flaves, bred up for that purpofe. But what is remarkable, neither Italian nor French mufic, vocal or inftrumental, makes the leaft impreffion on them; their organs, or their conceptions, are not accommodated to fuch founds; it feems to affect them like hearing an unknown language.

THE women's great accomplifhments are finging and dancing; the men look on them as congenial to the fex; but they are practifed in private only, amongft themfelves, fimply as domeftic amufements, or to pafs an idle hour. In many *Harems*, indeed, I have heard that they embroider and fpin.

THE Grand Seignor often diverts his ladies with a variety of recreations.
In

In the month of May they have the great Tulip-feaft, which requires vaft preparations. There are in the gardens of the Seraglio large parterres of variegated tulips, which, on thofe days, are interfperfed with all kinds of finging-birds; fhops are erected round them, and furnifhed by the Grand Seignor with all forts of trinkets, toys, and rich ftuffs: fome of the moft facetious females of his court are the fhop-women; he buys from all, and regales all his ladies: at night the whole machinery is decorated with lamps, and makes a pleafing profpect even at a diftance.

GREAT men indulge their women with the like amufements, and on thefe occafions of feftivity fome call in neighbouring *Harems*; fo that, perhaps, the women pafs their time more happily and

20

and agreeably than we imagine, or at
leaſt enjoy more health and vigour
than if they had operas, plays, Rane-
lagh, Vauxhall, balls and routes,
continually preying on their conſtitu-
tions, and abridging a ſhort exiſt.
ence.

WINE is ſeverely prohibited by their
religion. Mahomet knew his ſectaries
too well to entruſt them with the uſe
of it; for they are ſtrangers to mode-
ration in their paſſions, and wine ſeems
to have a different effect on their conſtitution, than on that of the reſt of mankind; it drives them generally to fury,
frenzy, and diſtraction. But notwithſtanding the prohibition, the vice of
drinking gains ground with the Turks,
and imperceptibly creeps from the
lower to the higher ſtations: perhaps,
in this inſtance, as in many other, re-
ſtraint

ftraint may quicken appetite and en-
flame defire.

MEN of fome diftinction, even thofe
in great offices, frequently make parties of what they call pleafure, merely
to get dead drunk; and after lying
two or three days wallowing in their
liquor, return frefh and happy to their
office.

A FREQUENT requeft to fuch Chriftians as they know they can truft, is
to procure them the beft wine. Some
principal officers, both in the Seraglio
and the Porte, have fo ftrong a paffion
for it, that they have invented fmall
leathern boxes, in which they convey
it home without the privity of their
truftieft fervants: and I have known
others fill large leathern pipes which
were pliant round their bodies, to carry

wine furreptitioufly into the Seraglio,
at the rifque, perhaps, of their lives.

WHEN it happens that towards the
decline of life, religious fcruples have
feized them, or that thofe in high office have apprehended the Grand Seignor might difcover them by the odour
of their morning's draught; they frequently change their wine to opium,
which is equally intoxicating, and perhaps attended with worfe confequences,
both to the corporeal and mental faculties. Some ftill continue that
practice; but at prefent thofe among
the great, who feel the fcruple
or fear the difcovery, rather betake
themfelves to diftilled ftrong waters, with which they are abundantly
fupplied from Zant and Corfu. The
cafuiftry with which they filence their
fcruples is, that fire, which purifies all
                                    things,

things, has, in diftillation, deftroyed and diffipated the impure parts of the wine; and that brandy is no where nominally interdicted by Mahomet. Thus they think they can diftinguifh away the *Koran*, cheat the devil, their prophet, and the Sultan.

THE vice of drinking wine is, however, looked upon with deteftation by the generality of Turks; and even the ufe of opium held a great difparagement, a defpicable practice. When they would depreciate the character of any confiderable man who is known to chew it, they call him a *Tiriachi*, that is, an opium-eater; by which they mean, a mind extravagant and irregular.

To give a diftinct detail of an object fo vaft and extenfive as the military eftablifhments in Turkey, is not in the

power

power of any mortal; I doubt whether any one man in their empire ever attempted it.

At Conftantinople there are an hundred and fixty-one *Oddas*, or chambers, of, or rather for, Janizaries, diftinguifhed by their numerical order, as our regiments are, faid to contain from eight hundred to a thoufand each; but thefe different chambers are never fully inhabited by that actual number. Moft of thofe whofe names are enregiftered as belonging to them, are difperfed throughout the empire, live as burghers mixed with the people, and follow different trades and profeffions.

The policy of Sultan Machmut, whofe principal ftudy and fupreme object was his own fecurity, has imperceptibly reduced that formidable body of militia,

militia, at leaft the part refiding at Conftantinople, into a ftate of quiet de-
pendance and fubmiffion.

All thefe *Oddas*, or chambers, ori-
ginally intended for no more than forty
thoufand, are fince that time augmented, and have at prefent, perhaps, * a
hundred and fixty thoufand men, or
more, belonging to them; but there are
never within their walls above eight or
ten thoufand. Thefe ferve for a guard
to the city, are formed to difcipline,
accuftomed to chaftifement, bending
to the ftick, ftrangers to the ancient fpirit of that foldiery, and are
permitted no other weapon than a
large taper club. If any of them
fhould be guilty of infolence, or attempt to be refractory, he is immediately

* The number of Janizaries throughout the
empire is reputed by fome to be 2 or 300,000.

dif-

difpatched either to a frontier garrifon
or to the other world.

THE pay is fmall; fo that many
who call themfelves of thofe chambers,
almoft difdain it : they receive the pay
indeed, merely to be confidered of that
corps, and to enjoy its immunities,
protection, and fupport.

THE duties, or cuftoms, are, properly fpeaking, farmed at Conftantinople, and throughout the empire.
The fubjects of thofe Chriftian powers
who are under capitulations, that is,
who have treaties with the Grand
Seignor, pay very low duties for goods
imported from Chriftendom; but the
Turkifh fubjects fufficiently compenfate
that difference : the officers of the cuftoms charge them at pleafure, according
to their will and caprice, eight, or ten,
and

and more in the hundred for whatever they import.

SULTAN Machmut, among other immunities, granted the Janizaries an exemption from thefe duties of importation. This has induced a furprifing number of them to engage in the moft lucrative parts of their coafting-trade; extending it even to Cairo, Syria, &c. and has effectually turned their martial into a commercial fpirit. Thus by promoting induftry, he hath introduced riches and luxury amongft them; fo that many of thofe veterans, who formerly rejoiced in the confufion of rebellions and revolutions, are at prefent anxious for the tranquillity of government, for the fake of their own fecurity and eafe.

H. 4.

In

IT does not follow, however, but that the provincial Janizaries, and other orders of soldiery on the frontier, would, at this day, appear as formidable in the field as they have ever been; at least there is reason to apprehend it from their behaviour the last war.

THE Turkish cavalry consists in a regular body of about thirteen thousand Spahis: these are divided under six standards.

THE pay of these two corps of infantry and cavalry, as it is distributed every six months at Constantinople, amounts to two thousand four hundred purses, of five hundred dollars each.

BESIDES these, there are the *Zaims* and *Timariots*, who hold feudal tenures, and are obliged, according to the value

of

of the feud, to appear in the field, each with three or four horfemen, or more, well mounted and accoutred. Thefe are good troops, and exceeding numerous.

We might add many other bodies of militia. There are the *Gebegys*, who have the care of the powder, ball, and all the ammunition for war: when they are complete, they fhould amount to four thoufand men.

The *Topegys* are the cannoneers, and have nothing elfe under their care but the cafting cannon, mortars, &c. and charging and levelling them : they form a body of two thoufand men.

The bombardeers are alfo a feparate body, entirely employed in the practice of throwing bombs.

This

THIS sketch of the military force of the Ottoman empire muft fuffice for the prefent ; fince what we do know befides, imperfect as it is, might fill almoft a volume. I juft mention thefe different corps, that I might give fome idea of the Turkifh power, and fhew, that in the military department, as in every other branch of government, the Turks obferve fixed regulations and eftablifhed order.

THE police of that great city of Conftantinople is admirable. The Janizaries, I have obferved, are the city-guard : with fingle clubs they keep all the inhabitants in fubjection ; no riots, no mobs, no diforders are known in the ftreets ; at the leaft noife the delinquents are fecured, confined, and punifhed.

In Sultan Machmut's reign, about thirteen Afiatic Turks, prompted by enthufiafm, or infpired with the fumes of opium, ran in a body through Conftantinople, exciting the people with moft vociferous exclamation, and unceafing uproar, to inftant rebellion, and exhorting them to raife their ftandard at the Hypodrome. They ftruck an univerfal terror through the inhabitants, the fhops were all fhut at once, and the outcry of a rebellion fpread itfelf over all the city. But thefe defperate rebels found none hardy enough, or fufficiently prepared, to join them. Their celerity was fo great, that the Janizaries could not reach them. They pierced without an obftacle into the *Bezeftyn*, or great Exchange. Moft of the fhopkeepers there are Greeks : their ancient fpirit arofe, or rather, their own fecurity obliged them to attack

the

the rebels. Armed only with the poles which fupported the fhutters of their fhops, they knocked down the Afiatic Muffulmen, who were all feized ; whilft the brave Greeks, terrified at their victory, quitted their fhops to feek an afylum, and to fecure themfelves againft the rigour of the law, for having, as they thought, murdered the true believers..

THE Sultan's equity, however, foon diffipated their fears, and put a ftop to any proceedings againft them. He publifhed, under the fanction of the *Mufti*, not only a free pardon to the Greeks, but full permiffion to his fubjects of any religion to deftroy all difturbers of the public peace ; he might have added, and of his own fecurity.

FALSE

FALSE weights are what the civil policy profecute and punifh with the utmoft rigour. The Vizir himfelf in perfon often vifits the fhops : the *Stambole Effendi*, or judge of Conftantinople, watches them affiduoufly. The bakers * are the moft frequent victims to the feverity of their juftice. If in any fhop they find bread that is fhort of weight, they mulct and baftinade the baker for the firft offence ; but the fecond or third, after a fummary procefs, produces a ftaple driven into the middle of his door-cafe, on which the offender is hanged; and it is not uncommon, as you pafs the ftreets, to rub againft a pendent Baker's body for three days fucceffively : it is, however, inconceivable, that almoft weekly examples cannot deter them from fraud.

* They are moftly Armenians who exercife this trade.

C H A P.

CHAP. XIII.

Obſervations on the Greeks.

THE modern Greeks are a near image and reſemblance of the ancient. Too crafty and ſubtle, too intriguing, vain, and vindictive, either to ſupport and maintain the intereſt, reputation, and glory of a republic; or to ſhare with, and ſubmit to govern-ment under a monarch of their own; their buſy ſpirit ſeems exactly formed and adjuſted to live no where tranquil but under a foreign ſubjection; where the heavy hand of power can depreſs the ſoaring ambition of their genius, and curb the violence of their paſ-ſions; where ſeverity can awe them to obedience, and if not to ſocial vir-tue, at leaſt to ſocial quiet.

THE

THE Turks have suffered them to retain some marks of honour, some traces of a former splendor; but these are entirely confined to the hierarchy of their church, and to three employments of profit and dignity in civil government.

THE former confifts in their four patriarchs, and, perhaps, one hundred and twenty other metropolitan bifhops; the latter in the two vayvodlicks, or principalities, of Walachia and of Moldavia; and the important office of *Drugoman*, or interpreter of the Porte, who is always a Greek, and through whofe hands all foreign tranfactions muft pafs.

THE Turks zealoufly fupport the Greeks in thefe remains of honour: they are a never-failing fource of wealth

6

wealth to the men in power; a fure profit, of which they can avail themfelves without danger.

WHOEVER could live among the Greeks, and obferve their refined intrigues, their eternal and continued contefts for thefe ecclefiaftical and civil dignities, would fee a true portrait in miniature of the worft Peloponnefian republics, and a moft ftriking refemblance of their abominable practices under their own emperors, from Conftantine to the laft of the Palæologus's.

A PATRIARCH of Conftantinople muft fpend among the Turks ninety or a hundred thoufand dollars, to obtain that dignity. He feldom lafts above three years: he is, during that time, continually ftudying to fecure himfelf on

his

his * throne. Several powerful Turks, his protectors, muſt have continual fees; he muſt devour the church to feed them; and in his precarious ſituation ſecure a conſiderable ſum to protect or reinſtate himſelf, after he is depoſed and exiled.

IF he acquires this ſupreme eccleſiaſtical dignity by favour of the Seraglio, the moment after his exaltation, his diſappointed adverſaries and competitors begin to undermine him, and contrive his ruin. Indifferent whether with truth or falſehood, they traduce and blacken him to the Vizir; ſtrengthening and ſupporting their truth or calumny with a powerful preſent.

* The Greeks call it the Patriarchal Throne; and they addreſs him by the title *Agiotate*, or, *Moſt Holy*.

IF the Porte patronizes him, and he has obtained the Vizir's protection, then they apply to the Seraglio, and attack him there with the fame arms.

OR if they have only the fame canal through which the patriarch obtained his advancement, from that moment they are daily fuggefting new caufes for his depofition.

DIFFERENT factions, which continually exift among the Greeks, unite together to effect his ruin, and jointly contribute to fupport the expence of thefe intrigues; and often perfonal hate or family enmity, but moft commonly interefted views cement the union.

THE Metropolitans, who generally refide at Conftantinople, exert all their art to circumvent each other; make ufe of every moment, and employ
every

every means, to depose a patriarch, or to get themselves promoted to a better bishoprick; and care not who they distress or ruin, provided they succeed.

HENCE there are continually some of them in exile. Sometimes the man whose money has had sufficient influence with some powerful Turk to procure his enemy's proscription, is himself in the same case the next day; for another Turk of superior weight, and actuated by the same motive, finds out and affords the banished man the easy means of retaliation: in short, these ecclesiastics are a constant lucrative game in the hands of the Turks, which they take care to play so artfully that it never ends.

A METROPOLITAN had fixed his eye on an archbishoprick, which he was determined to have at any price. Dur-

ing

ing the life of the archbifhop, all his at-
tempts were in vain; though, in good
truth, the archbifhop's character was
fuch, as might furnifh abundant reafons
even for a Turk to depofe him.

At length the archbifhop had a pa-
ralytic ftroke; he dropt fuddenly down,
and was thought dead. Preparations
were made for his funeral. The grand
ceremony is to feat the dead prelate in his
pontifical throne, dreffed in his pontifical robes; while he thus fits in ftate,
two chaplains attend at the door of the
room, where all of the Greek religion
are admitted to pay their laft duty to
him, and to kifs his hand: they think
it a meritorious act, a kind of religious
duty.

The time allotted for this ceremony
was elapfed, the moment approached
for his interment, the coffin lay at the
fide

fide of his throne, with all the requifites
for finally clofing it up, when fome of
the principal men amongft the Greeks
who could not attend before, earneftly
preffed his two chaplains for admittance
into the room, but were told it was
then too late. They perfifted, however, in their requeft; and though the
ufual hour was paft, fuch was the importance of thefe pious vifitors, the
chaplains dared not refufe. One of them
advanced before the company; and as
he approached, the archbifhop opened
his eyes, cried out for a glafs of water,
and afked, what meant that difmal ap-
paratus of the coffin? Surprize and
aftonifhment feized prieft and people;
they ran out of the room in amaze:
the other chaplain, after fome hefitation, boldly adventured, crofs in hand,
to approach the archbifhop, adminiftered
to his wants, and fatisfied his enquiry.

Dur-

DURING the interval in which the report of the archbishop's death prevailed, the Metropolitan applied to the slave of the *Kislar-Aga*, and offered to pay him down immediately six thousand zequins for the archbishoprick. All was agreed on, the money was paid, and the command from the Porte, which is their Congé d' Elire, was to be immediately made out. A few minutes after, news being brought to the Metropolitan that the archbishop was recovered, and alive, he went in haste to the slave, and begged for his money again; but the slave told him with a grave and composed mien, it was the same thing whether he paid it then, or some time after, for the archbishop could not live long; counselled him to remain quiet; and promised, that although he would in the mean time keep the money, the Metropolitan might look up-

on

on himſelf as heir-apparent to the arch-
biſhoprick. The Black, his ſlave, and
dependants, fell a ſacrifice to the publick two months after the archbiſhop's
reſurrection, who lived, however, two
years after, to laugh at the folly of his
pſeudo-ſucceſſor, who, in fact, never
ſucceeded.

But the arts, practices, and intrigues
among the clergy are trifling, when
compared with the extent and profun-
dity, the labour, toil, and perſeverance
of thoſe carried on among the preten-
ders to the Vayvodlicks of Walachia
and Moldavia; they ranſack heaven
and earth for means to deſtroy each
other.

There are always, when two are in
power, two or three of the depoſed
who are endeavouring to be re-in-

I. 4   ſtated.:

ftated : they fpare no coft ; they have the purfes ready of many expectants, as well as of their own dependants, who have fhared the plunder of thofe countries with them before ; or if that is not fufficient, they promife the fum required, which they may fecurely do ; for when once they are named, they find money at twenty-four for the hundred intereft, altho' it often happens that the principal is never repaid.

It has been known that they have difburfed, at the moment of taking poffeffion, from * fifteen hundred to two thoufand purfes of money to the Porte.

The intrigues they carry on have been fo deep and dangerous, that they have coft many, even opulent, Greeks

---

* Ninety-three to an hundred and twenty thoufand pounds.

their

their lives, which they have miferably finifhed in a halter at their own doors. A Frank refiding at Conftantinople, who threw himfelf as a dependant on a depofed Vaywode, and who thought himfelf fufficiently protected, ventured to fend a fcheme to his correfpondent in Moldavia for exciting that people to rebel againft the Vaywode in poffef-fion, accompanying it with fevere re-flections on the Turkifh government; he fent it by what he efteemed the fe-cureft conveyance. His letter, not-withftanding his precaution, was inter-cepted, and he loft his head near the Seraglio: no follicitations could fave him.

THE revenues of thefe principalities are racked to an inconceivable height. The princes juftify that oppreffion by the conftant demand from the Porte:

their

their purfes muft be ever opened, or they are inftantly depofed. Thofe of Walachia are faid to amount to three thoufand purfes the year, but moft people think it nearer four. Moldavia is faid to produce feventeen hundred purfes; but is eftimated nearer two thoufand five hundred.

THE contraft obfervable between the behaviour of thefe mock princes in power, and out of it, fhews the dege-neracy of the Greek character in a moft glaring light. Oftentatious pride, empty vanity, contemptuous infolence, acts of tyranny and oppreffion, attend their profperity: Depofed, you fee them dejected, pliant, bafe, groveling, even to moft abject fervility. I have known them carried before the *Stambole Effendi*, or judge of Conftantinople, for debt, and deny their own hand-writing.

THEY

THEY are seldom depofed without imprifonment or exile, and being ftripped of a large fum; but when they throw forth more of their ill-gotten wealth into Turkifh bofoms, they appear again at large; and, often, foon after remount the throne.

WHATEVER arts and fciences, whatever virtues might have been found in ancient times among the Greek republicans, feem to have been obfcured, or totally loft, under their emperors. The prefent Greeks have not a trace of them remaining. Their ancient language, or the literal Greek, as they call it, is a dead language: when they do underftand it, they have learned it at fchool.

THE art of healing, fo neceffary to the human fpecies, fo much cultivated,

and

and so highly honoured in ancient Greece, seems to be no farther considered among the present race than as one of the fairest means of introducing themselves to the favour of Turks in power, and a species of traffic, by which they may with most probability expect to advance their fortune : the best of them are strangers, I fear, as much to the integrity, as to the abilities, of their great countryman Hippocrates.

AMONG the many practitioners in physick at Conftantinople, are some few of the Greeks who have studied at Padua with tolerable success ; but the greater number are absolutely ignorant of the first principles of the art: they have most of them taken no other degree than what is conferred on them by the mere *fiat* of the *Echim Pafhi*, or chief physician

cian to the Grand Seignor. This they obtain for a small fee: it authorizes them to open a shop; and thus qualified, they think themselves avowedly privileged to sport with the lives and purses of their unfortunate patients. Shops are the diploma to practice; the sale of drugs, good or bad, must furnish them with subsistence; for the Turks are strangers to giving fees, excepting to physicians under ambassadorial protection, and who have no shops: even then their fees are bestowed very sparingly.

A GREEK physician of some note, finding himself in a time of pestilence unable to retreat into the country for want of money, set his wits to work how to provide it: they are fertile in resources on such occasions. A Turk of high rank and great opulence had an only son,

son, who happened juſt at that time to have a ſlight indiſpoſition, occaſioned by the eruption of a great boil. The Doctor, working on paternal tenderneſs and paternal fear, ſoon perſuaded the father it was the plague, tho' he hoped of the leſs malignant kind. The father, alarmed, intreated and conjured him to undertake his cure. The phyſician, appearing to be ſeized with horrid apprehenſions, heſitated, doubted, and at laſt told him, that he knew but one poſſible method to enſure ſucceſs, which was by adminiſtring the Bezoar ſtone, if he could by any ways and means procure it; for that it was extremely difficult to be found, and exceſſively dear. The father preſſed, intreated, conjured, that he would obtain one at any rate. The phyſician feigning great anxiety and perplexity where, and how to find it, left him with ſeem-

ing

ing defpair of fuccefs; pretending to
go and feek for it: he returned, as
if he had miraculoufly found one,
though he had it in his pocket before.
He had purchafed it for ten fhillings,
but he demanded of the Turk twenty-
five pounds as the loweft price, and it
was paid him. The cure fucceeded, and
the phyfician retired to the country,
boafting of his great abilities, which
had fupplied his immediate neceffity
by fo ingenious, and, as he thought,
laudable an expedient.

ANOTHER phyfician, of more eminence in his time, gave out, that he
could at all times command pregnancy
in women by an infallible arcanum;
that though he had made the difcovery with great ftudy and expence, he
would not conceal it; for as no other
phyficians had it in their fhops, he was

the

the only one could fupply the afflicted
with it ; that, in fhort, it was fimply
pure lion's urine. Buyers flocked
to him ; he prepared his own urine,
and fold it at an extravagant rate. If
complaints were brought him that the
medicine did not fucceed, the excufe
was at hand ; it was always fome fault
either in the time or manner of admi-
niftring his medicine : he knew that
with women he could not be admitted
to correct either.

Any common fervant to a phyfician
of any tolerable reputation, after a few
years fervice, were it only in beating at
the mortar, or even in carrying about
drugs, thinks himfelf fufficiently fkilled
in the medical art to ftand on his own
bottom, and kill by diploma.

I have known a Greek of great
eminence and practice much favoured
by

by a Vizir; yet this Doctor could not write.

THE Armenians, with feeming ponderous ftupidity in their countenance and make, are yet, as to all animal wants, as fubtle and defigning a people as the Greeks.

THEY are reckoned the beft grooms in Turkey; and by the care they take of a horfe, feem to have fomething in their nature congenial with that animal. One of them, who had ferved many years in that capacity, advanced his ftation by being admitted as a menial houfhold fervant to a private gentleman. His mafter fell into a languor, and though long attended by an able phyfician, died.

AFTER his death, the Armenian, difdaining fervitude, fet up for a phyfician.

HE was obferved one day going to a Turk of great diftinction, attended by feveral fervants, and treated with uncommon refpect. The queftion being afked who he was, it was anfwered, An eminent Armenian phyfician.

SOME time after, one who knew him, expoftulated with him on his infolence and temerity; and afked him, where, and by what means he could fancy he had learned phyfic? how he dared expofe his own life, which would be forfeited, the firft Turk his ignorance fhould kill?

HE anfwered, he had fufficiently learned that art from the phyfician who formerly

formerly attended his mafter; and who he was certain adminiftred medicines with great caution; that as he had obferved his mafter, in moft difor-ders, occafioned by colds, had made ufe of warm punch, of which the Doctor alfo ufually partook, he had, for that reafon, conceived a high opi-nion of it, had tried it on him-felf with fuccefs; and therefore, he limited his prefcription to that medi-cine only; and as it was exceedingly agreeable and palatable to the great men who employed him, and gene-rally fuccefsful, he was amply reward-ed for it.

THE city of Conftantinople actu-ally fwarms with fuch wretches, or rather, indeed, worfe: they are, it is thought, increafed within thefe forty years to above a thoufand.

If

IF the modern Greeks are almoſt ſtrangers to the virtues, or to all arts and learning of the ancients, they have ſurpriſingly retained their levity. Without the leaſt knowledge of Homer, Anacreon, or Theocritus, they abound in poetry, ſuch as it is, love-ſongs, ballads, and paſtorals; they are eternally ſinging or dancing.

THEY have carefully preſerved the Cretan Lyre, and Pan's pipe, the *ſeptem imparibus calamis*, " ſeven unequal " reeds," and alſo the pipe of the Arcadian Shepherds.

THEY ſtill uſe the ancient long dance led by one perſon, either with women alone, or intermixed with men and women, called by pre-eminence the *Romeika*, or Greek dance.

THEY

THEY have alſo the manly martial Pyrrhic dance, and thoſe moſt obſcene infamous love-dances, accompanied with the *Ionici Motus*, offenſive to all modeſty and decency.

CHAP.

CHAP XIV.

On the religion of the Greeks.

BEFORE I difmifs the Greeks, I fhall take fome notice of the ftate of religion amongft them, and produce fome facts to illuftrate what I advance.

THE name of Chriftian, which they profefs, with great conftancy, under the oppreffion of Turkifh government, has induced us to commiferate their fufferings ; while their abhorrence of popery, and the unremitting hate with which they are perfecuted by the Romanifts, has recommended them to Proteftants of every denomination; and has perfuaded us, that their religion has a refpectable fhare of purity both in its doctrines and practice.

ABOUT

ABOUT the time of the Reformation, and more especially in the reign of James I. even thofe inclined to Puritanifm entertained a favourable opinion of the Greek church. Cyrillus Lucaris, patriarch of Conftantinople, had almoft perfuaded archbifhop Abbot, that his doctrines did not differ from perfect Calvinifm. The patriarch meant no more by this, than to obtain the favour of the Englifh court, and the protection of their ambaffador at Conftantinople; fuppofing it the moft probable means of fecuring himfelf from the violent perfecution raifed against him by the minifters of the Roman Catholic powers, who, at that time, with the moft affiduous activity, and at a prodigious expence, in fupport of their own miffionaries, attempted the fubverfion of the Greek church; but it muft be acknowledged, that he

K 4　　　　　gave

gave a very falfe account of his religion.

It is with great reluctance that I repeat the melancholy truth, but it is the truth, the Greeks, like fome other fects of Chriftians, have entirely neglected to cultivate the genuine practice of true religion : they feem to have forgotten thofe real, and perhaps, only terms, on which mortals can render themfelves acceptable to the Deity; that purity of manners, brotherly love, forgivenefs of injuries, juftice in our dealings, and thofe other Chriftian duties every where inculcated in the gofpel of Chrift ; while the name of religion is folely appropriated to the firm belief of certain myfteries, and the regular practice of various external acts of humiliation and worfhip, with a ftrict obfervance of many auftere fafts

and

and rigorous mortifications, which at best can be only intended as the means by which to facilitate our approach to practical Christian perfection.

HENCE it is, that the Greeks seem to look on the eternal laws of social and moral virtue as the shadow only, and the arbitrary injunctions of their church, as the very essence of Christianity; and they think to compound for the total neglect of the first, by a rigid observance of the latter; insomuch that a Greek of the most depraved manners would suffer almost any thing, sooner than break a religious fast: the Armenians, indeed, surpass them in the number and austerity of these fasts, and in the strictness of their abstinence.

ALTHOUGH the love of money is not less predominant with the Greeks than

than with the Turks, yet their purses are ever open for the support of the eccle-siastical dignity, the building and de-coration of their churches, and the maintenance of their claims to the ex-clusive possession of the holy places in Palestine, against the Romanists, who make the like claim.

At the accession of Sultan Musta-pha, their present emperor, the Greek churches were in a ruinous condition; one of them had been almost entirely burnt down: the Mahommedan law does not permit new churches to be erected; even large repairs are prohi-bited. On the birth of the Sultan's first child, the Vizir suggested to his So-vereign what kind of favours he should confer on his different subjects, during the ten days appointed for the rejoic-ings on that great event, so important

to

to the peace of the empire. Amongst others he mentioned, as a most acceptable indulgence to the Greeks, a permission to repair that church which the fire had almost destroyed: he durst not ask leave to rebuild it, though there was scarce a wall standing. The Grand Seignor condescended to grant them the ten days for that repair. No sooner was this known, but every Greek mason and labourer quitted all his other work, and flew to contribute his assistance at the church: two or three thousand men constantly relieving each other, the whole was accomplished, and the church rebuilt, in less time than was allowed for the repair, and that without any one disbursing a sixpence. The only reward the workmen received for their indefatigable labour was conscious merit, and the priests blessings. Let this suffice for an instance of their zeal.

I would wish to throw a veil over the scandalous contentions which have been carried on between the Greeks and Romanists on account of Bethlehem, and the Holy-Land, as it is called: the iniquitous proceedings attending them are so enormous, as shamefully to disgrace the Christian name. The ambassador who protects the interest of the Romish religion, becomes, on these occasions, notwithstanding his high dignity, a real object of compassion.

Immense sums are raised in all the countries of the Romish persuasion, to support them against the Greeks, in their pretensions to a spot of ground which they fancy sacred; and to preserve in the hands of popish monks and friars the remains of an old stable at Bethlehem, where a chapel is built, and

in

in which on the authority of an uncertain oral tradition they fuppofe Chrift was born ; and alfo a fepulchre, which may, but moft probably may not, be what they call it, his fepulchre : the exact fituations of both places, are at prefent as unknown, as that of Julius Cæfar's urn.

WHY the princes of Chriftendom will fuffer their countries to be defpoiled of fo much wealth, and permit it to be paid on this account, as a tribute into the hands of the Turks, is hardly conceivable ; and why no angel has flown, or fwam, acrofs the fea with this fepulchre, or this manger, as with the houfe at Loretto, is yet a greater wonder. Princes, it fhould feem, ftill permit this tribute to be paid to the Turks, becaufe they have thought it beft to leave this bufinefs as they found it ; and not chufing

ing to meddle with what are called religious matters, fuffer the clergy to go ftill on with the fame practices as prevailed in the times of the darkeft ignorance, and the moft extravagant fuperftition. At prefent, few or no pilgrims of the Romifh perfuafion refort to thefe places of devotion. So that the moft probable reafons to be affigned for the attachment of their clergy to the poffeffion of them are, that it occafions much money to pafs thro' their hands, and that it affords a maintenance for about an hundred and fixty idle monks and friars who are diftributed about that country.

In the conteft between the Greeks and Romanifts for the right of poffeffing the chapel at Bethlehem, and the ftable, treafures have been expended by both parties, to the great emolu-

7   ment

ment of the Turks, who take care, from time to time, to fpirit up the difpute, giving fentence fometimes in favour of the one, and fometimes of the other. Under Ragib Pafha's government, it was finally determined in favour of the Greeks, at an expence equivalent at leaft to 10,000 l. fterling.

THE Holy Sepulchre has been, and ftill is, as great an objeƈt of contention between them, and a prodigious, annual expence to both.

BUT what is worfe, the Turks knowing the riches and obftinacy of thefe contending parties, find numberlefs other pretences to pillage their wealth. The caravan for Mecca paffes near Jerufalem. When it approaches that holy city, the *Emir Hadge* either enters

in

in perſon, or ſends a meſſage to demand a loan from the Greek and Ro-
miſh convents; or, perhaps, on ſome
pretence of right, to exact a ſum of
money, 20, or 30,000 l. ſterling from
each party: they dare not refuſe. If
it be a loan, it is never repaid; if on
a pretence of right, be it ever ſo
groundleſs, the ſum is irrecoverably
loſt, and never heard of more.

THE Greeks behave with much pru-
dence on theſe occaſions; they ſtifle
their complaints, bear the loſs, and
immediately repleniſh the fund, that
they may again be in a condition
to combat the *Paſhas* and the Romaniſts: they would even ſell their
children rather than permit the latter
to triumph over them.

THE

THE ambaſſador, whoſe peculiar charge it is to protect the Romaniſts, wears out his very ſoul in fruitleſs application at the Porte to recover the ſum of which his convent has been ſtripped. With much difficulty he may obtain the Sultan's command in his favour, that is, an order for reimburſement; but it procures him no money; and what is more vexatious, he is frequently impoſed on, by the miſrepreſentations and downright falſities of theſe prieſts and monks eſtabliſhed in Paleſtine, who are continually peſtering him with ſlanderous accuſations againſt the Greeks: he is officially bound to ſupport them; and after ſuffering in his credit at the Turkiſh court, by the mortifications he is obliged paſſively to bear, when theſe falſities are detected; he is, nevertheleſs, reviled at Rome by the whole

body of clergy, as a lukewarm Chriftian, and an unfkilful politician.

The Greek fyftem of religious opinions and their mode of worfhip, is
pretty generally known. They agree
with the Romanifts in the main points
of the doctrine of the corporeal pre-
fence, their veneration for faints, and
the adoration they pay to the Virgin
Mary; in their image-worfhip they
differ: they honour paintings, but al-
low of no fculpture. The proceffion of
the Holy Ghoft is another, and moft
important article of diffenfion; they
hold it is from the Father only. And,
they fcoff at the pope's pretenfions to
infallibility, and at his claim to be
fupreme head of the univerfal Chtiftian
church. Their clergy give no previous
difpenfation for the omiffion of any religious duty, but referve the abfolution
of

of all tranfgreffions and fins till after they are committed.

ABSURD and fuperftitious practices abound among them, and frequent abufes happen, the natural concomitants of uninformed credulity, not peculiar to the Greeks only : one of a fingular nature was carried on a few years ago, by a *Caloyero*, or monk. He had fome years before been noted for his irregular and profligate life, and had been in the gallies at Conftantinople. On being releafed, he affected an extraordinary degree of fanctity, and enthufiaftic fits of devotion. If he did not lay claim to the higher gifts of miraculous powers, he at leaft pretended to have celeftial communications, and to be endowed with the peculiar grace of enfuring to ancient women, happinefs in the world to come ; and to

the

the young and middle-aged women, the happiness of this world, children. Barrenness is looked upon in Turkey as a curse: women who bear no children are hardly treated with common civility; the sovereign good and honour therefore of every married woman in that country, is to be a good breeder. The hope of becoming mothers, it may of course be imagined, led shoals of unhappy females to the new faint; the privileged dispenser of pregnancy.

He established himself at Caterlee, a village in Asia, to which you pass by water in a few hours from Constantinople; his emissaries were dispersed through all the neighbourhood, and wherever they went, spread the fame of his sanctity and his marvellous gifts. Devotees flocked to him: it was reckoned that eight thousand women,

of

of different ages, ran, in a fhort time,
to participate of fuch defirable graces.
The faint was a ftout faint, of a middle
age, and never failed to fend away his
female votaries perfectly edified.

Some men at length vifited him, and
feemingly approved his proceedings;
not that they really believed in
his pretenfions to fanctity, but becaufe they would not, by publifhing
their fufpicions, caft the leaft fhadow
of injury on the character of their
women. They wifhed the fterility of
their wives removed, but they apprehended the means might be difagreeable
to themfelves. The journey was pleafant, the paffage by water convenient, and other adventures might co-
operate with the faint's fpiritual endeavours. Hints of this were given
to the Turks, who foon made this

im-

impoſtor decamp. He was not heard, of afterwards. He did not, however, quit his vocation empty-handed; for the conditions of approaching him was the purchaſe of a conſecrated wax-taper, beſides a free-gift; in both which articles, religious zeal, and the deſire of becoming mothers, had en-gaged the good women to pay moſt generouſly.

The Greek religion, I am, how-ever, told, is better ſupported, and maintained with greater purity, on its primitive foundation in other coun-tries where it is profeſt, undiſturbed by Mahommedans or Romaniſts. Nor would I be thought to mean, that there are no ſelf-denying Metropoli-tans, and other honeſt men, even a-mongſt thoſe in Turkey.

F I N I S.